A Sister's
secret

A Sister's Secret

Two Sisters. A Harrowing Secret.
One Fight for Justice.

DEBBIE GRAFHAM

with **HEATHER BISHOP**

EBURY
PRESS

1 3 5 7 9 10 8 6 4 2

First published in 2014 by Ebury Press, an imprint of Ebury Publishing
A Random House Group company

The Random House Group Limited Reg. No. 954009

Addresses for companies within the Random House Group can be found at
www.randomhouse.co.uk

A CIP catalogue record for this book is available from the British Library

The Random House Group Limited supports the Forest Stewardship
Council® (FSC®), the leading international forest-certification organisation.
Our books carrying the FSC label are printed on FSC®-certified paper. FSC is
the only forest-certification scheme supported by the leading environmental
organisations, including Greenpeace. Our paper procurement policy can be
found at www.randomhouse.co.uk/environment

Printed and bound by CPI Group (UK) Ltd, Croydon, CR0 4YY

ISBN 9780091958442

To buy books by your favourite authors and register for offers visit
www.randomhouse.co.uk

*For my brother, David, for giving me the courage
to speak out. I kept your promise in the end.*

*And to my little sister, Laraine,
who has been there with me every step of the way.*

This book is a work of non-fiction based on the life, experiences and recollections of me, Debbie Grafham. In some cases names of people/places/dates and sequences of the detail of events have been changed to protect the privacy of others. The names of Patrick Ryan's family have been changed to protect their identities. This happened to me over thirty-five years ago. Some of the details described are, of course and happily, blurred by time. Other details – and in particular the incidents Patrick Ryan was convicted of at his trial – are, sadly, as vivid as if they happened to me yesterday.

Contents

Prologue

It's three in the morning and something has woken me. I sit bolt upright in bed and look around at the strange surroundings. It takes me a few minutes to remember that I'm staying the night at my father-in-law Eddie's house. The only familiar sight is my husband, Rob, lying next to me, and he's snoring his lugs off.

My head aches and my stomach churns with dread as I remember what day it is. The 23 April 2013. An ordinary, mundane Tuesday morning to most people, but there was going to be nothing routine about today for me.

Slowly I climb out of bed trying not to wake Rob, and creep downstairs to make a cup of tea. It's not even light yet but I go out into the garden. My hands shiver in the cold of the early spring morning as I light up a cigarette.

'You're going to be fine,' I say to myself as I take a sip of tea. 'He can't hurt you any more.'

I tell myself the same thing over and over again. Perhaps if I say it enough times I might actually start to believe it? I know I don't feel fine, far from it.

Another cup of tea, another cigarette but it's still only 4am. Six hours to go. I really should try and get some more sleep but my heart is pounding and that familiar, overwhelming feeling of panic grips my body. Diazepam, I think, that's what I need. That always helps. I go back upstairs, get into bed and twist the top off the plastic bottle. I quickly swallow one of the little blue tablets then I close my eyes, willing it to hurry up and take effect.

But there's no escape. As I start to relax into sleep the words hit me like a bolt of lightning.

'Keep your fucking eyes open.'

'No,' I want to shout. 'I don't want to look.'

Stifling my sobs, I pull the duvet up around me for protection.

'Open your eyes, you little whore,' I hear the voice in my head say again.

And all of a sudden I'm nine years old and I can feel him on top of me again, the smell of his stale, beery breath against my neck.

'No,' I scream. 'I don't want to.'

Opening my eyes, I realise that I'm still in bed with Rob asleep beside me. I take a deep breath and try and stop myself from shaking.

You're OK, you're safe, I say to myself.

The green glow of the digital clock on the bedside table tells me it's 5am. Five hours left to go. Thankfully the Diazepam has finally kicked in and I can breathe properly, but my heart is still pounding and those awful words are ringing in my ears.

'Open your fucking eyes.'

These are the words that have broken me, devastated me and kept me awake endless times over the past 35 years. The words that send me into a cold sweat. You see, I didn't want to keep my eyes open; I didn't want to see what was happening to me. If my eyes were closed then I thought perhaps I could pretend that it had never really happened.

But it had.

Six o'clock. It's daylight now and I'm longing for Rob to wake up so I will have someone to talk to and reassure me. I can see my new clothes hanging on the wardrobe door. A black jacket and trousers, and a white blouse. Smart, safe, business-like. All neatly pressed for the umpteenth time.

'Look smart, Debbie,' the police had told me.

I thought that if I looked respectable then perhaps it would help disguise the feelings of shame and disgust that consume me.

It's 6.30am now. I shuffle around a bit, cough a couple of times and thankfully it's enough to make Rob stir, and I'm no longer on my own. He sees me sitting bolt upright in bed.

'You OK, Deb?' he asks.

'Yes, love,' I lie.

It's not long before my mobile starts beeping with text messages.

Good luck Debbie. Thinking of you. You can do it, you'll be OK.

But I don't reply to any of them. I'm frightened that if I do then they'll know that I'm not OK, that I'm falling to pieces here.

7am. Only three hours to go and I'm wide-awake now. It's time for a shower. The shower is my sanctuary. The place where I spend hours each day trying desperately to scrub away the feelings of disgust and self-loathing.

'Come on, Deb,' I hear Rob shouting up the stairs. 'Come and get some breakfast.'

God only knows how long I've been in here. It's almost like I'm in a trance. Still on autopilot, I dry myself and get dressed in my new clothes that feel completely alien to me compared with the jeans and trainers I normally wear.

'You look smart,' says Eddie as I go downstairs.

Even though I might look good on the outside, inside I'm a wreck. My stomach is churning with nerves and I don't want to sit down in case I get my clothes creased.

'Have something to eat,' says Rob.

But I never eat breakfast and especially not today, when I feel sick with nerves.

More cups of tea. More cigarettes. I know I'm putting everyone else on edge with my endless pacing up and down, but I just can't sit still.

My mobile beeps with another text message. This time it's from my little sister, Laraine. The only other person in the world who knows exactly how I'm feeling today.

Deb are you OK? I'm scared.

This is the one text that I do answer.

You'll be fine Lal. You'll be OK. Just stay strong and I'll see you soon.

It's just before 9am now. Time to go soon. The Diazepam has well and truly worn off. My stomach is churning and my hands are damp with sweat. I know I shouldn't take another one as I have to be alert and they make me drowsy, but my whole body is shaking and the room is spinning. In the end I give in and have a half just to take the edge off.

'We'll leave at 9.15am,' says Rob.

'Can't we go any earlier?' I say. 'Can't we go now?'

Time is dragging and it's torturous.

'We'll be way too early, Deb. We'll leave here at quarter past.'

He puts his arm around me, safe and reassuring, as always.

'Rob, I'm scared,' I say. 'I can't do this.'

'You'll be OK,' he replies. 'I'll be with you. You can do this.'

But the tears that I've been holding back all morning suddenly come tumbling out. I've tried so hard to keep it together and stay strong but the reality is I'm a wreck. The memories that I've kept buried for so long suddenly feel real again.

'I'm sorry,' I say, taking a deep breath.

'It's OK, Deb. You'll be fine, I promise,' Rob tells me.

But I just nod.

'I'd better go and wash my face,' I say.

I go upstairs to the bathroom and stare at my reflection in the mirror. I've never worn make-up, so at least there's no mascara to run, but my eyes are all red and puffy from where I've been crying. How, nearly 36 years later, could I be reduced to this? How could one person still fill my heart with so much fear and dread?

I give my hair a quick brush and go downstairs again, where Rob and Eddie are waiting.

'It's time,' says Rob. 'Are you ready?'

Am I ready? Am I really? I don't think I'm ever going to be ready to reveal the deep, dark secrets that I've kept hidden for the past 35 years. This is the day that I've been waiting for so long, yet the day I've also been dreading.

But Rob is right, it is time. Time to face the monster who has destroyed mine and my sister's life. Time for the world to know all about the despicable things that he did to us. It's time for us to make him pay, and hopefully get justice at last.

Chapter 1
Behind Closed Doors

A banging and clattering from outside the front door made us both jump. Mum and I looked at each other in a panic. We knew it could only mean one thing.

Daddy was home.

'Quick, get to bed, Debbie, it's late,' Mum muttered under her breath.

'No, Mummy,' I said. 'I told you I was going to stay up.'

We could hear swearing as my father tried and failed to get his key in the lock. Then the ching of metal hitting the ground as he dropped it onto the floor.

He'd been gone for two whole days and by the sound of it he'd spent most of that time at the pub. 'On one of his benders' was what Mum used to call it and even though I was only four years old I knew exactly what that meant.

I could see the worry in her eyes.

'Please, Debbie, go to bed. I can deal with your dad.'

'No, Mummy,' I said. 'I promised I'd look after you.'

I knew all too well what was about to happen as it went on so often. I'd hear loud voices first, Dad shouting and swearing, finally followed by Mum's screams as he laid into her. Sometimes I lay there on my top bunk with my hands over my ears trying desperately to block it out. Other times if I was feeling brave, I'd run onto the landing and peep around the banister. If he was going to kill her, I reasoned, then at least I could run down there and try and stop him. But I always closed my eyes at the sight of my lovely mummy being punched, slapped and kicked. She didn't just stand there and take it, though. Often she tried to fight back: in fact one night she'd broken her hand trying to hit him.

In the morning it would all be quiet and calm, like nothing had happened. Dad passed out on the settee, Mum making breakfast, wearing a long-sleeved top so we couldn't see the fresh purple bruises on her arms.

No one ever said anything. Not me, nor my brother David, aged three, or my sister Laraine, two. Our baby sister, Davina, was just a few months old, mercifully too young to know what went on in our house. All of us were too little really to understand it. I thought that's what everybody's mummy and daddy did, but I still knew I didn't like it.

As the eldest I felt it was my job to protect Mum, so tonight I'd decided that I was going to be there if Daddy came home. With his key finally in the lock, the door flung open and he staggered into the room. That strong, funny smell that Mum always said was beer hit my nostrils and made me feel sick.

'What the fuck is she doing up?' he slurred when he saw me.

'She's just going to bed, aren't you, Debbie?' Mum told him.

'No, I ain't,' I said defiantly. 'I'm staying up to make sure that you're nice to Mummy.'

Dad laughed.

'I'll show you nice, you little bitch,' he said, lunging towards us.

But it was Mum he was going for and she yelped as he slapped her round the face, leaving an angry red mark on her cheek. I ran over to Mum in my long flowery nightie and stood in between her and Dad.

'Please Daddy, don't hit Mummy any more,' I pleaded.

There wasn't much chance of a four-year-old fighting off a fully-grown man but I was determined to try. I saw a flash of anger in his brown eyes and he started to undo the belt from around his trousers.

'Daddy, please love Mummy,' I said.

'Get to your bed or I'll thrash the living daylights out of you,' he threatened.

'Don't you dare touch her,' shouted Mum. 'Debbie, go to bed. Please, love,' she pleaded.

Her voice sounded desperate now. I knew if I didn't then it would only make it worse for her in the end, so I rushed up the stairs to my bedroom.

My sister Laraine was still awake. She was sat up in the bottom bunk, her eyes wide with fear.

'Sshhh, it's OK, Lal,' I said, stroking her soft black hair. 'Go back to sleep.'

But I knew neither of us would sleep while we could still hear the sounds of our mummy's screams downstairs.

My dad, Fred Fermor, was an alcoholic and my mum, Maureen, suffered from depression. I suppose you could say it was a match made in hell from the start. They'd met in a psychiatric hospital after Mum had had a breakdown and Dad was being treated for a personality disorder. Dad worked as a farmhand but he was always getting sacked for not turning up or for stealing and we moved all around the South East. Since I was born we'd lived in Eastbourne, Orpington and Brighton and now we were on a farm in Burgh Heath, Surrey. Mum hated our farmhouse, which came with Dad's job and was in the middle of nowhere. It was dark, damp and dingy, and there was hardly any furniture in it.

But when Dad wasn't drunk, to the outside world he could be very charming. His mother was Sicilian and he had tanned, swarthy skin, dark-brown eyes and jet-black hair that he slicked back with Brylcreem. He wasn't particularly tall but he was strong with big muscly arms from all the heavy lifting he did on the farm. He always made an effort to look smart and even if he was only going down to the local pub he would wear a suit and a shirt with a ruffle down the front, which was very fashionable at that time in the 1970s. He would always be clean-shaven and he would douse himself in Old Spice.

Sometimes he was even nice to us kids.

'I've got a special treat for you, Princess,' he told me one day.

'What is it, Daddy?' I asked.

I loved animals and I was always begging him to take me with him when he was working on the farm.

'As you're the eldest, I'm going to teach you how to milk a cow,' he said.

I felt so special as I held his hand and skipped along next to him towards the barn. I watched, fascinated, as Dad showed me how to gently but firmly squeeze the teats until the milk came spurting out.

'There's a bit of a knack to it,' he said. 'Now you have a go. Don't be scared, she ain't going to hurt you.'

The cow seemed massive to me but I did as Dad said and I was proud as punch when I saw the warm milk squirt into the silver bucket.

'You've done good, Debbie,' he said.

That's when I decided that I loved animals so much I wanted to be a vet.

Dad even took us on a day trip to the seaside once. It was one of my best memories and sometimes when things were bad at home I would close my eyes and relive that day at Westgate-on-Sea: Mum's smiling face, Dad buying us ice creams and us kids digging for hours in the sand with our buckets and spades. Just for one day I had felt like any other family. Normal. Ordinary. Happy, even.

But the nice times were few and far between. Mostly Dad would make promises that he couldn't keep and he would go off to the pub and never come back. Sometimes we wouldn't hear a peep from him for days, weeks even.

Mum did her best but she was left on her own in the middle of nowhere with four of us kids and no money. Her family, especially my Granddad George, hated my dad. He lived in sheltered accommodation in southeast London, so it was hard for him to come and visit us; we didn't see a soul.

I didn't know the word for it at the time but Mum got more and more depressed. I knew she was sad as she was crying a lot, and eventually it all got too much.

Dad had done one of his disappearing acts and had been missing for days. One afternoon I was playing dolls outside in the fields with Laraine. We loved our battered old plastic dollies that Mum had bought us in a charity shop and we spent hours pushing them around in an old, rusty toy pram. When we came back in, Mum was sat on the floor of her bedroom in floods of tears.

'Oh Debbie, your father's been back and taken all of my clothes to give to his fancy woman,' she sobbed.

I didn't know what a fancy woman was but I could see that Mum's wardrobe was completely empty.

'He's taken all of the food vouchers too,' she wept.

I knew this was bad news. Every week the Social would give us food vouchers which Mum would use at the local shop. She needed them to feed us all as she could never rely on Dad, who would normally spend his wages in the pub.

'Don't cry, Mummy,' I said. 'You can borrow some of my clothes if you want.'

At least that made her smile.

That night as Laraine and I went to our room, I noticed Mum sat on her bed taking her tablets. For as long as I could remember, she always had a brown glass bottle that the doctor had given her on her bedside table. She had a blank look on her face as she calmly popped pill after pill into her mouth.

'Night night, Mummy,' I said, but it was like she was in a daze and she didn't reply.

The next morning I woke up. Normally Mum would be up first, making us some breakfast, but the house was eerily quiet. I went into her room but she was still asleep. Davina was lying next to her in her cot, babbling away.

'Mum, can we have some toast?' I asked.

She didn't stir.

'Mummy,' I said, tapping her arm. 'Wake up. I'm hungry.'

By then David had come in too.

'Mummy looks funny,' he said.

Now I was really starting to panic. She was all floppy like a rag doll and I just knew something was wrong.

'Please wake up, Mummy,' I said, shaking her as hard as I could.

She started to moan and drool dribbled out of the corner of her mouth.

Suddenly I heard the front door go and Dad sauntered in, like he'd just been to the shops. I ran to the top of the stairs and shouted, 'Mummy won't wake up.'

He rushed up, took one look at Mum and picked up the empty bottle of tablets lying beside her on the bed.

'Jesus, she's taken the bloody lot! I'd better phone 999,' he said, his face ashen.

The next few hours were all a blur. I remember an ambulance pulling up outside. David, Laraine and I huddled on the stairs in our pyjamas while paramedics rushed up past us to Mum's bedroom. Dad paced up and down, holding Davina who was howling.

Eventually they carried Mum out on a stretcher.

'Where are you taking her?' I asked them. 'Is she going to die?'

Nobody answered. Dad took Davina with him and followed them to the hospital in his old blue Humber.

By then a man had arrived who said he was a social worker.

'What's one of them?' I asked.

'Your mummy's not very well so I'm going to take you somewhere else to stay until she gets better,' he explained.

He helped me pack a little bag for each of the three of us. Just a few clothes as we didn't really have many toys. He led David and me to his car, leaving Laraine looking out of the front window, tears running down her face. She looked how we all felt – frightened, bewildered, confused.

'What about my sister?' I asked the social worker as he started the engine. 'Can't she come with us too?'

He shook his head.

'I'm afraid your foster mother can only take two children at a time, so Laraine is going to your aunt's in Gillingham.'

David and I held hands on the back seat. It felt like we were driving for hours and eventually we pulled up outside a brick terraced house. It was a lot nicer than anywhere we had ever lived but not one single part of me wanted to be there.

'You're going to stay here with Mrs Mason for a while,' said the social worker, letting us out of the car.

He rang the doorbell and waited. David looked terrified.

'Don't worry,' I told him, squeezing his hand. 'She might be kind.'

But there was nothing kind or welcoming about the woman who opened the door to us. She was smartly dressed in a flowery blouse and skirt with a checked apron over the top but I thought that she looked like a witch. She had a thin, pointy face and her mousey brown hair was scraped back into a ponytail. She didn't say a word to us, and she and the social worker went into another room to talk.

'Well, I suppose I'd better take you to your room,' she said finally when he'd gone.

We followed her up the stairs to a bedroom. It had nets on the small window as well as thick curtains and it seemed so dark. There were flowers everywhere – on the wallpaper and the curtains, and even the bedspreads on the two single beds had a chintzy floral pattern on them. It made me feel dizzy.

'I want my mummy!' sobbed David.

'Well, she isn't here and I don't want any moaning,' she said. 'If you're going to make a fuss then you can stay in your room.'

We sat there for hours until it got dark. David cried the whole afternoon.

That night a man came in to see us. He was a tall, stocky bloke with a bushy dark beard and moustache.

'This is my husband,' Mrs Mason told us. 'Say hello to him, children.'

'Hello, Mr Mason,' I said.

'Oh no, child, we would like you to call us Auntie and Uncle,' she insisted.

David just scowled.

'I'm hungry,' he told her.

We hadn't eaten anything all day.

'Well, you've been very naughty, carrying on and making a fuss, so you two will be having tea on the stairs.'

She led us down the steep wooden staircase which had an orange and brown paisley runner on it. We sat down at the bottom on the garish carpet.

'No,' said Auntie. 'Sit on the wooden bits either side.'

She gave us a marmalade sandwich each and went into the front room. As we sat on the hard, wooden stairs, shivering with cold, I could see her and Uncle through a crack in the door. They were sat around a huge dining table, tucking into some sort of stew that smelt delicious.

I was scared and miserable but I knew I had to be brave for David's sake. That night I couldn't sleep because I was so worried about Mum. Was she dead? Would we ever see her again? Was Laraine OK?

I could hear David sobbing.

'I want Mummy!' he wept.

'Come and sleep in my bed, Davey,' I said and we cuddled up under the scratchy sheets.

Time passed so slowly and every day was the same. Auntie would make us sit in our bedroom all day. We didn't have any toys to play with or anything to do and the curtains were always closed, so we never saw daylight. I'd never felt so sad. Auntie would bring us up a plate of marmalade sandwiches twice a day. That was unless she said that we'd been naughty and then we had to sit on the stairs for hours.

We'd been there a week, I think, when one evening Auntie came into our bedroom.

'I thought I would read you both a bedtime story,' she said kindly.

She carried David across to my bed and she sat in between us.

'That's what my mummy does,' I told her.

Auntie had a big book of nursery rhymes and she read us one about some children called Jack and Jill. Maybe she's not so bad, I thought.

The next night she came in and read to us again. This time she had a book called *The Famous Five*. It was about four children who went on lots of adventures and my favourite bits were about Timmy the dog.

'Thank you, Auntie,' I said. 'I love doggies.'

Perhaps she did like us, after all. One evening Auntie came into our bedroom for stories wearing a long nightdress and a pink quilted dressing gown. I didn't think there was anything odd about this as we were in our nightclothes, too.

This time she got into bed with us rather than sitting on top of the flowery quilt.

'Oh, Auntie loves you both so much,' she said.

I closed my eyes and pretended it was Mum putting her arm around us and not Auntie.

The following night she took off her dressing gown and long flowery nightie before the stories started.

'Auntie, you'll get cold with no clothes on,' I told her.

'Well, we'd all better cuddle up then to keep warm,' she said, getting into bed with David and I.

She snuggled up to us and read us a story.

'I love you both so much,' she said afterwards.

Suddenly I felt her hands rummaging beneath the sheets and I realised she was touching me under my nightie.

'Auntie, that tickles,' I said at first.

But I was frozen with fear as her cold hands wandered from my tummy to down between my legs.

'Auntie loves you both so much,' she said, turning her attentions to David.

I was four years old. I didn't understand what was happening but I knew I didn't like this touching game. David and I were too scared to say anything.

Another evening Auntie was in bed with us when Uncle came in. The door to our bedroom was a big double door with a panel at the top and I saw his piggy eyes and bristly moustache peering through the glass at the three of us. He must have just got in from work because he was wearing a suit.

'Oh look, Uncle has come to say goodnight, too,' she said.

David and I watched confused as he took off his jacket, trousers and shirt until he was stood there in his white string vest and purple paisley underpants.

He got into the bed with us.

'Have you had a lovely story, children?' he said, pressing himself up against me.

'Please, Robert,' Auntie told him. 'Don't hurt the children. Let me do it.'

'No, Ruby, it's my turn,' he said. 'Why should you have all the fun?'

Then to my horror, I realised he was touching me and then David too. He was rougher than Auntie and he had fat hairy fingers like sausages that really hurt me when they poked and prodded inside me.

We were both terrified. Afterwards David stayed in my bed, shaking like a leaf.

'I want to go home,' he told me.

'Me too,' I said.

This happened night after night. It was always the same routine. Auntie would come in first for stories and Uncle would arrive later. He did things to me that hurt so much I was almost grateful when it was just Auntie doing the touching.

One night I even thanked her.

'Thank you, Auntie, for not letting Uncle hurt us,' I said.

She smiled and said, 'You know we're only doing this because we love you.'

Afterwards, without saying a word, they would calmly get dressed and walk out. It was miserable. The days were so long and boring but I dreaded it getting dark because that meant it would be time for bed.

'I don't want no stories, Deb,' David would tell me.

But we were both too scared to say that to Auntie and Uncle.

One morning, when we had been there for two months, Auntie came into our bedroom.

'Come with me,' she said to David and I.

She led us down the landing into a tiny box room. There was hardly any furniture in there except a tatty wooden cot in the corner and stood up in it was a little girl.

'Laraine!' I yelled.

David and I were so pleased to see our little sister and she gave us a big grin. She'd always been small for her age but she looked so tiny and frail.

'She's been very unhappy and refusing to eat at your aunt's so the social worker thought she might be more settled here,' Auntie told us.

I was so happy to see her but at the same time my heart sank. Please don't let them read stories to Laraine, I prayed. She was two years old, practically a baby.

But we didn't see much of Laraine. Auntie wouldn't let her come into the bedroom with us during the day. She had to stay in her cot in her room. Sometimes we could hear her crying and one afternoon, I couldn't take it any more.

'I'm going to check on Laraine,' I told David.

'Auntie will be cross,' he said.

But I didn't care. I just needed to know that my baby sister was all right. As I crept across the landing, my heart thumped out of my chest as I heard Auntie in the kitchen downstairs.

Poor Laraine was just stood there in her cot. It was freezing cold but all she was wearing was a terry-towelling nappy which was so heavy with wee, it was hanging down to her knees.

'It's OK, Lal,' I said, giving her a kiss. 'Don't cry. We're only down the hall.'

Laraine smiled but her big brown eyes looked so sad.

'Mummy,' she said.

'I know, I want Mummy, too,' I told her.

Every day I hoped and prayed that we would see Mummy again but Auntie wouldn't answer any of my questions. I didn't know where she was or if she was alive or dead.

But I was the eldest and I knew that I had to be brave for David and Laraine. I would only cry when I was sure that David was asleep, then I'd let the tears fall until my pillow was soaked through and my eyes were puffy and swollen. I hated this place and I hated Auntie and Uncle and everything they did to us. I was terrified, too. Terrified that we would never see Mum again and that we'd have to stay here forever. Would we ever get out of here and go home?

Chapter 2

Going Home

It was three long months before we finally received a little ray of hope.

Auntie came into our bedroom one morning and said, 'I'm taking you to see your mother today.'

None of us could believe it, we were so happy. I was just relieved that she was still alive. I was allowed to go and tell Laraine.

'We're going to see Mummy, Lal,' I said, picking her up out of her cot and swinging her round.

Her little face lit up. Poor thing must have been so confused by everything that had happened to her.

Auntie drove us there in her orange Austin Allegro. It seemed to take forever before we pulled up outside a big brick building that she said was called Redhill General Hospital. We walked down lots of corridors until we got to a big room full of people. They were all sat in chairs chatting and there amongst them I spotted Mum with Davina lying next to her in a yellow carrycot. I couldn't believe it was really her. She looked happy and Davina had got so big.

'Mummy!' I said, running over to her.

We were all crying by the time she threw her arms around us.

'I've missed you all so much,' she said, showering us with kisses. For the first time in months, I felt safe.

'Did the doctors make you better, Mummy?' I asked as Laraine clambered onto her knee.

She smiled and said, 'Much better, darling. They've given me some medicine and I've had a good rest.'

There was so much I wanted to tell her about Auntie and Uncle, the marmalade sandwiches and the horrible bedtime stories. But Auntie insisted on sitting with us in the visitor's room, her beady eyes never leaving us for a second.

'Daddy's been writing to me in hospital and he said he's going to get us a new house,' Mum told us. 'It's going to be in London, near to Granddad George. Won't that be nice?'

Even the thought of having to live with Dad didn't dampen my spirits as long as we were far away from Auntie and Uncle and back with Mum again.

'Did you like the parcels I sent you?' Mum asked. 'I know you all love sweeties and I put some colouring books and pencils in there so you could do some drawing, Debbie.'

I was about to tell her that we'd never got any parcels when suddenly Auntie jumped up.

'Right, time to go now, children, your mother needs to rest,' she said.

I saw the panic in Laraine's face.

'*No!*' she screamed, clamping her arms tightly around Mum's waist. 'Stay with Mummy.'

Auntie had to literally drag her off Mum's knee as she kicked and struggled with all her might. I didn't want to go either, but I was too scared to say anything.

Mum started to cry.

'I'm so sorry. I love you all so much and it won't be long until the doctors say we can be together again.'

She gave us all a hug and a kiss before Auntie ushered us out. I took Laraine's hand and I literally had to drag her down the corridors and out to the car. She was crying so much, she could barely breathe. Her and David sobbed all the way home but I just felt numb. I missed Mummy so much and as we pulled up outside Auntie's house, I felt sick.

I didn't want to go back there. I didn't want to sit in that bedroom hour after hour, dreading it getting dark because that meant it was time for stories.

'You've all been so naughty you can go to bed without any sandwiches,' Auntie told us.

But I didn't care any more. I was too sad to even feel hungry.

When you're four years old you have no concept of time but it felt like we had lived with Auntie and Uncle forever. Being in that house had affected all of us. David started to stutter so badly that he stopped talking altogether. Laraine became more and more withdrawn and would sit in her cot, hardly making a noise. I tried to be brave for the two little ones but it felt like I had a big knot in my tummy that wouldn't go away.

One day Auntie took us out to the local shops, which only happened once in a blue moon. Even though it was a cloudy day it was nice to be outside in the fresh air, away from our flowery bedroom prison. Auntie pushed Laraine there in a blue and white pushchair but on the way back, she put her shopping bags in it instead.

'You'll have to walk,' she said to Laraine.

'Pushchair,' said Laraine, pointing at the buggy but Auntie shook her head.

'I said walk,' she told her.

Laraine started to cry and stopped dead in the middle of the pavement.

'Want pushchair,' she said, stamping her feet.

I could see Auntie was furious and she marched over and kicked her hard up the bottom. Laraine fell over and landed head first onto the cobbles.

'Leave my sister alone!' I shouted, rushing over to see if she was OK.

Poor Laraine had cut her head and was beside herself. Auntie marched us all home without saying a word. As soon as the front door closed, she lost it.

'Get up to your room,' she yelled at Laraine. 'And you two sit on the stairs until I say you can move.'

David and I sat there for hours. When Uncle came home he ignored us.

'What's the little one done to her head?' I heard him ask.

'Oh, the stupid girl fell over on the way back from the shops,' she told him. 'It's just a graze.'

We sat there for so long that eventually David wet himself. Auntie was furious that he'd peed on her stairs and we were sent back to our bedroom in disgrace.

One morning Auntie came in to see us and I noticed that she was carrying the checked holdalls that we'd brought with us when we'd first arrived.

'You're going back to your mother and father's today,' she said matter-of-factly.

I couldn't really believe what I was hearing. Was she playing a nasty trick on us?

'Is that man taking us home?' David asked.

'No, I am,' she said. 'Come on, pack your stuff.'

That only took a few minutes as we hardly had anything. I still didn't believe it, even in the car.

'We're going home to see Mummy,' I heard David say to Laraine. 'Daddy might be there this time.'

Laraine just stared into space and didn't react. She was so withdrawn now it was as if she had just switched herself off from normal life.

I didn't know where 'home' was any more but eventually we pulled up outside a big Victorian building. The new house Dad had promised us turned out to be a scruffy three-bed council flat in Abbey Wood, southeast London. But I didn't care, especially when the front door opened and I saw Mum and Davina, who was crawling around by her feet.

'Fred, they're back,' I heard her shout.

'Yay, Daddy's here!' yelled David, running in.

Even though I was in no rush to see Dad, I took Laraine inside as I wanted to get as far away from Auntie as possible. I heard her chatting to Mum on the doorstep.

'If ever you need me to take the children again, then I'm more than willing,' she said.

I never wanted to see that woman again and I didn't dare believe that she had really gone until I stood at the window and watched her drive away.

Dad was full of it.

'My beautiful girls,' he said when he saw Laraine and I. 'We're going to be a proper family again. It's a new start for all of us.'

I could tell Mum was on edge. She always was when Dad was around.

The new flat was cold and damp and the wallpaper was peeling off the walls but at least we were safe. Laraine and I shared a big bedroom with a door that led to the back garden.

Mum said we had been at Auntie and Uncle's for six months but believe me, the memories of living in that house have lasted a lifetime. None of us ever talked about it. David and I didn't have the words to explain what had happened to us and I prayed Laraine was too little to remember.

I tried desperately to forget but sometimes when I closed my eyes at night I'd dream that Auntie was in bed with me and I'd wake up screaming. Mum never asked us about it – I think she felt guilty about the suicide attempt and she just wanted to forget that time in her life.

I still had that knot of anxiety in my tummy and for months afterwards I was always on my guard, half expecting Auntie or a social worker to turn up and take us away again.

Laraine and I were asleep in our bunk beds one night when I heard tapping on the door in our bedroom that led to the garden. I ignored it at first but eventually it got louder and more persistent. I was absolutely petrified.

It's Auntie and Uncle come to get us, I thought.

'Who is it?' I asked, not daring to even open the curtain. 'My mum won't let you take us away.'

'It's Daddy, for fuck's sake,' said a voice. 'The bloody front door was locked and no one could hear me knocking so I thought I'd sneak round the back.'

He'd been at the pub as usual but as Dad staggered in, I'd never been more relieved to see him in all my life.

We might have all been back together again, but it was never going to be happy families with Dad around. The fresh start didn't last long and soon he was up to his old tricks – drinking and disappearing for days on end. He'd found work as a removals man and sometimes he did painting and decorating.

'Too much temptation for a light-fingered so-and-so

like him,' Mum would say, even though I didn't know what she meant.

But as usual, Dad would always turn up like a bad penny and try and charm his way back. One afternoon he came home with a big smile on his face.

'Mo,' he shouted. 'I've got a present for you.'

He made such a big deal of getting all of us kids to close our eyes as he carried in this big thing hidden under a blanket.

'Ta da!' he said, revealing his big surprise. 'It's a sewing machine. You was saying you wanted one for ages, so I thought I'd treat you.'

I could see Mum was pleased. For once he'd actually bought her something that she'd find useful. But her smile soon disappeared the following day when two policemen turned up on the doorstep.

'We're here to see Freddie,' they said.

'He's at work at the minute,' Mum told them.

'We think your husband's been helping himself to a few things that aren't his,' one of the officers explained. 'We need to come in and have a look round.'

Mum was close to tears as they searched the flat for stolen goods and turned everything upside down. Half an hour later they left with her new sewing machine and a copper kettle Dad had also brought home.

'Tell Freddie we called, won't you?' they said.

'But Mummy, that's the sewing machine Daddy got you,' said David.

'Your silly father took something that belonged to someone else,' she told him.

Nope, there was only one man in my life who I trusted and that was my mum's father, Granddad George. He was absolutely lovely. Every week he would come on the bus from his sheltered accommodation in Charlton to see us. Laraine and I would wait at the front gate for him and our eyes would light up when we'd see him walking down the road in his long grey mac, carrying a holdall that we knew was stuffed full of goodies.

'Some presents for my big girl,' he would say to Mum, giving her all of the things we could never afford, like fresh fruit, vegetables, cheese, bread and milk. 'And some Minties for my little ones.'

He would hand each of us a packet of Polo mints and a 10-pence piece. Laraine and David would be itching to spend their 10 pence straight away. We'd all go down the road to Tom's Sweet Shop and they would buy a penny mix-up – a bag of all sorts of sweets like Black Jacks and lemon sherbets. But I was happy with my Polos.

'I'm saving my money for a dog,' I told Granddad.

When we got home, I'd carefully put my silver coin into the little china piggy bank that I kept safely in my bedroom.

Granddad would also tell us stories. I loved sitting on his knee and hearing all about Mum when she was a little girl and her dog, who was called Judy. The other thing about Granddad was that he absolutely hated my father. In fact, if he knew Dad was going to be there he wouldn't come round.

He had good reason, we all did. By the time I'd turned five, I had started at the local primary school at the end of our road. Dad had been missing for a week when I got home one time, to find Mum in tears.

'He's been back and taken everything again,' she sobbed.

Dad would always take whatever he could find – money, toys, clothes, jewellery, food – anything he could sell to get some cash to spend on drink.

I could see he'd been in mine and Laraine's room this time. All of our drawers were spilling open, our socks and pants scattered over the floor. My heart sank when I realised what was missing.

'My piggy bank,' I cried. 'He's taken my piggy bank!'

Eventually I found it smashed on the floor in the front room. All of the money Granddad had given me that I was saving up for a dog with had gone. It was probably only a few coppers but it was *my* money and I was heartbroken that he'd stolen it. From then on I kept my money hidden in my glasses case in my drawer under a big pile of clothes.

With Dad taking what little money we had, it was a constant struggle for Mum to feed and clothe us. I remember skipping along beside her to the post office one day. We'd go there every Tuesday to collect her Family Allowance, which would give us enough money for the weekly food shop.

'I'm really sorry but I can't find my allowance book,' Mum told the woman behind the counter. 'Did I leave it here last week?'

She looked confused when Mum gave her her name.

'Oh, that's funny, your husband has already been in this morning to cash it,' she said. 'He said you were poorly so you'd sent him to collect it.'

I could see Mum's face drop. She was relying on that money to get us through the week.

It was the same with the rent on our flat. Dad told Mum he would pay it directly from his wages but a few months later someone from the council came round to say we were hundreds of pounds in arrears. Mum had no alternative but to find a job, so she started cleaning houses. She could take Davina with her when we were at school and she was paid cash in hand.

When I turned seven, the damp in our flat was so bad that we were moved to a new place in Coleraine Road, Blackheath. It was in a nicer area, in a big Victorian terraced house divided into two flats. We had the one downstairs with the back garden. Like everywhere that we had lived, it was shabby. We never had nice things, just a few bits of old, worn furniture that Mum had been given or we'd bought from charity shops. The walls were all painted the same drab shade of beige and there was no central heating except an electric heater in the front room, so it was freezing in winter.

David had his own room. Davina, who was two now,

still slept in a cot in with Mum and Dad, and me and Laraine had our own room. But the best thing about our new flat was the neighbours.

Living above us were a lovely couple called Estelle and Ian and they had four children who were exactly the same age as us kids. Mum got on well with Estelle, their eldest daughter Peggy was two months older than me; Barry was David's age, Susan was five, like Laraine, and Douglas was a toddler, like Davina. We'd all play in the communal front garden together and they would come into our back garden. We were in and out of each other's houses so much, we kept our front doors unlocked.

We all went to the same primary school down the road. I loved school as I saw it as an escape from my troubled home life but Laraine hated it and she struggled to settle.

Ever since we'd come back from the foster parents, she'd been quiet and withdrawn. The only people she would really talk to were Mum and I and she was terrified of strangers. She was still a tiny little thing and she hardly ate.

Sitting in class one afternoon writing a story, a teacher came in to get me.

'We need you to come and help with your sister,' she told me.

I could hear Laraine screaming as soon as I set foot in the corridor. She was in the girls' toilets, completely hysterical.

'What happened, Miss?' I asked her teacher.

'Your sister had a bit of an accident but when I tried to change her, she went like this,' she said.

When Laraine saw me, she fell into my arms, sobbing.

'She don't like no one touching her,' I explained. 'I'll do it, if you want.'

'Come on, Lal,' I said. 'Let's get you out of these wet pants.'

Mum was called up to school many times because the teachers were so worried about Laraine.

'Is there any reason why she's so withdrawn?' I'd heard a teacher ask Mum. 'Is there anything wrong at home?'

But the truth was nothing had ever been right at home. Dad was up to his old tricks, drinking, disappearing for weeks on end, then turning up and hurting Mum.

'Failure to thrive' the authorities had called it and eventually Laraine was sent to a special school for maladjusted children in Downham. Every morning a bus would pick her up and take her there, but it didn't stop her being a target for the local bullies.

As she stumbled in the front door one afternoon, I knew something had happened to her. Her dark, curly hair was all matted and her pink T-shirt was wet with tears and dirt.

'What is it, Lal?' I asked.

'The b-boys down the road were waiting for me when I got off the school bus,' she gulped between sobs. 'They called me a spacca for going to a special school and they said I-I-looked like Bugs Bunny because my teeth stick out.'

She was crying so much, her frail little body was shaking.

'They pushed me over and I cut my knee,' she sobbed, showing me the bloody red patches seeping through her thick white tights.

I could feel the anger bubbling up inside me.

'No one speaks to my little sister like that,' I said. 'Where are they, Lal? I'll go and sort them out.'

'You ain't gonna get them now, Deb, they ran off,' she said.

Trust the bullies to pick on the weakest. Laraine wouldn't say boo to a goose and she'd never hurt anyone.

I'd have done anything for my little sister. I'd failed her once at Auntie and Uncle's when I hadn't been able to stop them from treating her so cruelly. Now I was determined nothing bad was ever going to happen to her again. But I didn't realise then what was in store for us. If only I'd known how far I was going to have to go to protect her.

Chapter 3

Summer of Hell

The bell rang and the hum of excited chatter and laughter filled the corridors.

'We're off to Margate for a week and we're staying in a caravan.'

'Well, *my* dad's taking us to Spain and we're going on a plane.'

It was the last day of school before the summer holidays and swarms of happy children ran to the gates, comparing notes about their plans.

But all I felt was a sense of dread because I knew there would be no treats or day trips or holidays for me. Just six long weeks of boredom while Mum went to work and we tried to keep ourselves entertained.

I waited patiently outside for my little brother, David. Most of the other kids had gone by the time he came strolling out.

'Last one out as usual,' I sighed, but he just flashed me a big grin.

'No more school for six weeks, Deb,' he grinned.

His excitement was infectious. Now that I was nine,

Mum had promised that she would let me go down to the local park on my own. That was something to look forward to at least.

'Come on, I'll race you,' David said suddenly before tearing off.

He beat me easily and waited at the end of our road for me to catch up. But as we turned the corner into our street, I saw something that filled my heart with dread.

A familiar blue car was parked outside our flat. A clapped-out old Humber.

My father's car.

David rushed up the front steps while I hung about outside, not able to bring myself to go in. A few seconds later he came flying out the door.

'Debbie, Dad's here!' he yelled, his face filled with happiness. 'He's inside. Come on.'

I walked into the porch and slowly took off my school shoes, putting off the inevitable for as long as possible.

'Dad says he'll take us to the seaside,' said David, his whole face lighting up. 'Isn't that brilliant, Debbie?'

'And you believe him?' is what I really wanted to say, but I bit my tongue as I could see how excited he was to have Dad home. His latest disappearing act had lasted three weeks.

So instead I took a deep breath and said, 'That's nice, Davey.'

He literally dragged me into the front room but I knew Dad was there before I even saw him. The smell of stale alcohol and roll-up cigarettes hit my nostrils as I walked through the door.

He was sprawled out on the sofa and, I was relieved to see, asleep. I turned to walk away.

'Hi, Princess.'

I stopped dead in my tracks and turned around.

'Hi, Dad.'

'Are you going to give your dad a hug?'

Reluctantly I walked over and sat down next to him. My body tensed as he put his arms around me.

'How are you doing?' he asked.

'I'm OK, Dad,' I said.

'Where's your mum?'

'She's out cleaning,' I told him.

'Well, I've got a couple of days off work so I thought I'd take you kids to the seaside.'

My heart soared. *The seaside*. Just like my friends. That would be something to tell everyone about in September.

'Will you really, Dad?' I asked. 'Do you promise?'

'Anything for you, my little princess,' he replied.

They were words that I'd heard a million times before and I knew his promises were always broken. Yet this time I so desperately wanted it to be true.

David wandered into the room again.

'I'm starving, Debbie,' he said.

'I'll make you a sandwich to keep you going until Mum gets home,' I told him.

David was always hungry and he ate like a horse despite being all skin and bone.

'I've got an idea,' said Dad. 'When your mum gets in, how about I go out and get us all fish and chips for tea?'

My mouth watered at the thought of steaming hot fish and chips, smothered in salt and vinegar and wrapped up in newspaper. We could never normally afford anything like that and it felt like it was Christmas.

'That'd be lovely, Dad,' I said. 'Do you promise?'

'Of course, love,' he replied. 'I've had a few week's extra work.'

He opened his wallet to show me a big bundle of notes. That would explain why we hadn't seen him for the past three weeks.

Before long, the school bus pulled up outside and dropped Laraine off. Her face lit up when she saw Dad and she threw her arms around him.

'How's my favourite girl?' Dad asked her.

I went into the kitchen and made him a cup of tea. Maybe he had changed. Maybe the summer holidays weren't going to be so bad after all.

'Here, Dad,' I said, handing him his cuppa.

'Thanks, sweetheart,' he said. 'I'm just going to go and freshen up before your mum gets home.'

He went to the bathroom and ten minutes later I heard the front door open. Mum was back: Davina was in her pushchair and there were bags of shopping hanging off the handles.

'Dad's home,' I told her.

I saw her whole body tense up.

'He's going to go and get us fish and chips, Mum,' said David.

'Is he now?' she sighed. 'How many times have I heard that?'

'He is, Mummy, he promised,' Laraine told her. 'And he's taking us to the seaside.'

Mum just rolled her eyes and started to put away the shopping.

'Where is he?' she asked.

'He's in the bathroom freshening up, then he's going down the chippy,' I said.

The weary expression on Mum's face said it all. How many times had Dad promised to do something and how many times had we sat there waiting? She'd had a lifetime of broken promises.

'Mum, I really think he means it this time,' I said.

But before she could answer, Dad came out of the bathroom. He was dressed in a nice shirt and a smart suit. He always took pride in his appearance even if it was just to go down to the fish and chip shop.

'Hello, Mo,' he said to Mum.

'Welcome back,' she replied.

She didn't even lift her head up to look at him.

'I won't be long,' he said, heading out of the door.

We sat down to watch a bit of telly. An hour went by but Dad wasn't back yet.

'Shall I get us something to eat?' Mum asked.

She made a sandwich for Davina and Laraine but David and I refused.

'Dad's bringing us fish and chips,' I said.

Another hour passed and there was still no sign of Dad. Mum ran us a Dettol bath. David and I got in first, then Davina and Laraine.

The two little ones went to bed but David and I stayed up. We waited in our pyjamas in the front room, not prepared to give up on the promise of fish and chips.

'He'll be back soon,' David told me as I stifled a yawn.

By 10pm my tummy was rumbling and I was shattered.

'I'm hungry,' moaned David.

Mum didn't say a word. By 10.30pm the telly had clicked off because the meter on the back had run out of ten pences.

'Right, bed,' said Mum.

David had fallen asleep by now so she carried him to his room.

'But Mum,' I said, 'Dad's getting us fish and chips.'

'How many times has he said that?'

'He will, Mum,' I said. 'I know he'll be back soon and he'll be cross if we've gone to bed.'

'It's 10.30pm, love,' she replied. 'He's not coming back.'

I could see she was angry. So I went to bed hungry but most of all disappointed, not with Dad but with myself for believing his promises again. After all these years, I should have known better. Eventually I drifted off to sleep.

Something had woken me. I looked at the clock: 11.30pm.

I heard a key in the door, footsteps staggering around in the darkness. Dad was finally home.

I turned over on the top bunk and pulled my flannelette sheets and yellow blanket over me while Laraine snored away in the bottom bunk. My tummy was still rumbling with hunger but it was too late now. Promises had already been broken.

I heard Dad knocking on his bedroom door. Angry with him and not wanting him coming in late and waking Davina who slept in there in her cot, Mum had obviously locked it.

'Open the door, Mo,' he yelled. 'I've got fish and chips.'

Too little, too late.

'Open this bloody door.'

But his pleas fell on deaf ears and Mum didn't respond. Then I heard footsteps coming along the hallway. A figure in the doorway.

'Hi, Princess, are you awake?' he said.

I shut my eyes and pretended to be asleep.

'Princess, Daddy's home.'

I didn't say a word. I heard him climb up the ladder to my top bunk and smelled the strong stench of alcohol and tobacco as he lay down beside me.

'Sweetheart, I've got you a present,' he said.

'Dad, I'm tired,' I sighed, turning away from him.

'I mean it, I've got you a present,' he said. 'Open your eyes and have a look.'

I opened them but the room was pitch black.

'I can't see anything,' I told him.

He took my hand and guided it to something warm and quivering at the end of my bed.

'I got you a puppy,' he said.

I was so happy and excited. I'd begged Mum for a dog for years.

'Please can I see it?' I asked.

'In the morning,' he replied.

'Please, Dad,' I begged.

'I said you can see her in the morning,' he told me. 'We can't put the lights on now, it will wake your sister.'

'I suppose so,' I sighed. 'Thank you, Daddy.'

'That's OK, anything for my best girl.'

My eyes were heavy with sleep, but I so desperately wanted to see my new dog.

'What colour is she, Dad?' I asked.

There was no answer, just the sound of snoring beside me. I knew I would have to wait until morning to find out, so I closed my eyes.

The sound of whimpering must have woken me up. It was still dark and Dad was passed out beside me.

'Dad, wake up,' I whispered. 'The puppy's crying.'

His arm was draped across me so I tried to lift it off. I knew he could hear me because the snoring had stopped.

'Dad,' I whispered.

'Shut up,' he hissed.

'Dad, I need to go to the toilet.'

'No, you don't,' he groaned.

'Dad, I do,' I said. 'And the puppy's crying. What's the matter with her?'

Suddenly I saw him sit up in the darkness. He took off his tie, unbuttoned his shirt and pulled off his trousers. I couldn't understand what he was doing.

'Come here,' he said, reaching out for me.

'No,' I said. 'I don't want to.'

I felt frightened although I wasn't sure why. Maybe it was something about the tone of his voice? It sounded like the way he spoke to Mum before he lunged at her.

'I said come here,' he growled. 'Don't you like your present?'

'Yes, I do,' I said.

'Well, come here.'

'Dad, I don't want to,' I told him. 'I'm going to the toilet.'

'No, you're not,' he said.

I tried to get to the top of the ladder so I could go to the loo but his arm yanked me back. I was terrified now as he knelt over me, holding me down on the bed.

'Dad, you're hurting me,' I whispered.

'I'm not going to hurt you,' he said.

His face was inches away from mine now and my body was pinned underneath him so I couldn't move. I flinched as I felt his hand lift my long cotton nightdress up, his fingers probing, digging, hurting. Just like Auntie and Uncle.

'Dad, stop please,' I begged.

His mouth covered mine, silencing me. All I could

taste was stale beer and cigarettes. I couldn't breathe, I couldn't scream. Then he lay on top of me and I felt an excruciating pain, a horrible burning sensation between my legs.

I tried to move but I couldn't and all the air was being squeezed out of my lungs as I felt the weight of him moving up and down on me. Eventually I felt him tense and at last he rolled off me.

I lay there, paralysed with fear. I couldn't move. I tried to say something but no words came out. I could hear whimpering again but this time I realised that it was me making that pathetic noise and not the puppy.

I heard a voice in the darkness.

'Sweetheart, I'm sorry,' he said. 'I'm drunk, I never meant this to happen. Please forgive me.'

He reached out to touch me but I flinched and he pulled his hand away.

'I'm sorry,' he said again.

I huddled up against the wall, desperate to get as far away from him as I possibly could. I lay there motionless as I felt him pull down my nightie from up around my waist. I heard the zip of his fly as he put his trousers back on, followed by his shirt.

'Goodnight, Princess,' he said as he climbed down the ladder.

I didn't answer. I couldn't. I just lay there, unable to take in or understand what had just happened.

I was nine years old. I didn't really know about sex

but as with what the foster parents had done to us, I knew what had just happened was very, very wrong. But this wasn't a stranger, it was my own flesh and blood.

I heard my sister stirring in the bunk below. Oh God, did she know? Had she seen what our father had just done to me?

'Laraine,' I called out to her. 'Lal, are you awake?'

But she didn't answer and thankfully I could tell that she was still asleep.

The light from the landing was on now and I could see the outline of my new puppy curled up at the bottom of my bed. She was a scruffy little thing, black and tan.

Only minutes ago I had been so happy and excited about seeing her. Now all I had was a sick feeling in the pit of my stomach.

She was no longer a gift, a present from Daddy. She was my reward and I had paid for her dearly.

I needed the toilet so badly but I was scared in case he was out there in the hall, waiting for me. I swung my legs onto the ladder and felt the cold metal against my feet. My legs were weak and wobbly and there was a sharp pain in my tummy as I hobbled to the door.

Thankfully there was no sign of my father as I crept onto the landing. I opened the bathroom door as quietly and as carefully as possible, praying it didn't creak like normal. Safe at last, I pulled the bolt across and turned on the light.

I looked at my reflection in the mirror, hardly

recognising the girl staring back at me. My face was pale, my eyes were red and puffy and my lips swollen. I sat down on the toilet, the seat cold against my skin. I was desperate to pee but I was too scared. Eventually I forced it out but the stinging was unbearable.

I sat there, still in shock. Was it my fault? Had I done something to make him do it? Had I said something wrong?

Was it only a few hours ago that David and me had sat happily playing in the bath, eager to get out and have our fish and chips? It all felt like such a long time ago now.

Wiping myself carefully with toilet paper, I winced at the pain. I could see the start of purple bruises on the inside of my thighs and as I stood up, a trickle of blood ran down my leg. I was scared and wanted Mum but what would I say to her? I couldn't tell her what Dad had done because I didn't really understand it myself.

I felt dirty and disgusting and I had an overwhelming urge to wash it all away. I filled the sink with hot water and looked around for some soap, anything to get the smell of him off me.

All I could find was some toothpaste so I squeezed the whole tube straight into my mouth. It stung but I didn't care. I saw the bottle of Dettol on the side of the bath from earlier and I tipped a load into the sink and watched the water turn cloudy. Then I got a flannel and scrubbed myself over and over again until my thighs were red raw and all I could smell was the overpowering antiseptic of the Dettol.

Slowly I opened the bathroom door and tiptoed across the landing. I passed David's room, where I could hear him snoring, and then went into my bedroom. Laraine was asleep and the dog was still curled up at the bottom of my bed. I climbed up the ladder and pulled the sheets over me, but they wreaked of Old Spice and cigarettes and it made me feel sick.

I tried to sleep but all I could hear were his words in my head.

'I'm sorry. I didn't mean it.'

Did I believe him or was it just another lie? Had he really meant to do that to his own daughter?

I didn't know what time it was but I lay there for what felt like hours. Eventually I heard the birds twittering and saw the first glimpse of dawn through the crack in the curtains.

The first day of the summer holidays. How was I going to carry on as normal after what had just happened? My whole world had changed and now I was going to have to face the man that had done this to me.

I must have dozed off eventually as I woke up with a start. Laraine's bed was empty now and I could hear Mum making breakfast in the kitchen.

Had I imagined what happened last night? Was it all just a bad dream? Then I heard it. A whimpering sound coming from the end of my bed, and I saw my dog properly for the first time.

I don't want a puppy, I told myself.

Because that meant what had happened last night, what my father had done to me, was all real.

She wasn't as small as I thought she would be. She wasn't really a puppy, either: she was a scrawny, bedraggled stray. She had a mark around her neck where her collar had rubbed and I could see her ribs sticking out from beneath her fur. I didn't want to love this dog as I knew she'd be a constant reminder of what he had done. But I knew it wasn't her fault and I could see that this poor neglected mutt needed me.

'Hello,' I said to her.

Her little ears pricked up when she heard my voice. Her tail wagged and her big brown eyes locked with mine. I reached out to stroke her but she cowered away, pushing herself against the metal foot of my bed.

'Come here,' I whispered, holding out my hand for her to sniff. 'I'm not going to hurt you.'

As soon as the words were out of my mouth I realised with horror that was exactly what my father had said to me, only hours before.

'Come here,' I said again. 'It's OK.'

I could tell the dog was scared, but in the end curiosity got the better of her and she edged closer. I gave her a stroke. She felt warm, soft and comforting. My heart went out to this little bedraggled dog who just wanted a bit of love and kindness because I knew exactly how she felt. And as she climbed onto my lap and I held her close, I couldn't stop the tears from falling.

Chapter 4
New Neighbours

I decided to call my new dog Judy, just like Mum had called her dog when she was a girl. I was so busy stroking her matted fur, I didn't even notice that Mum had come into my bedroom.

'Oh, you're awake,' she said. 'I've done you a bit of toast.'

But I didn't want breakfast and most of all I didn't want to have to face that man. I couldn't even bring myself to call him Dad any more.

'I ain't hungry, Mum,' I said. 'I don't want no breakfast.'

'You must have something, love,' she said, reaching up to give Judy a stroke.

'Your dad said he'd got you a dog. At least he kept one of his promises, eh?'

I nodded. If only she knew what he'd taken in return.

Eventually I summoned up the courage to go into the kitchen. Thankfully there was no sign of Dad and I prayed that he'd cleared off back to the pub again. I got my toast and walked up the four steps leading to the front room, where we had a dining table in the bay window.

Davina, Laraine and David were sat there tucking into toast and jam and, to my horror, Dad was sprawled out on the old blue sofa asleep. He was fully clothed in his shirt and suit and he'd even put his tie back on.

I felt sick to my stomach at the sight of him. My hands were shaking as I picked up a piece of toast.

Just act normal, I told myself. Pretend he's not there.

I took a bite of toast but as I tried to swallow it, the bread got stuck in my throat and I retched. I ran to the bathroom, where I was violently sick.

Nobody had noticed, but I knew that I couldn't even be in the same room as him. I was frightened about how he was going to react to me and I was terrified of Mum finding out.

The one place I felt safe was in the bathroom because it was the only room with a lock on the door, so I got dressed in there. Afterwards I was in the kitchen giving Judy some water when Dad walked in.

'I promised I would get you a puppy, didn't I, Princess?' he said.

I stared at the floor, not able to even bring myself to look at him.

'Shall we take her down the park for a walk?' he asked.

I just shook my head. He walked towards me but I started to edge away until I was pressed against the back door.

'I'm so sorry, Princess,' he said, lowering his voice. 'I was drunk. I didn't know what I was doing.'

I didn't say a word. I tried to get past him but he got his wallet out of his pocket and handed me a pound note.

'What's that for?' I asked.

'Go buy the dog a collar and lead,' he said.

'I don't want your money,' I replied, pushing his hand away.

He left it on the side and walked out. I was shaking like a leaf and I felt like bursting into tears.

It was only years later that I realised Dad couldn't have been that drunk if he'd remembered everything so clearly the next day. He'd managed to get his key in the front door, climb up the rickety little ladder to the top bunk and back down again, where he'd got himself dressed. I'd seen him in far worse states, when he was so paralytic that he'd just pass out in the hallway. To this day, I still believe that my father knew exactly what he was doing.

I know what you're thinking. Why didn't I say anything? Why didn't I tell Mum or my granddad? But I was nine years old and I was scared. I knew Mum would be upset and it would cause rows between them and that Dad would take it out on her. Imagine if he killed her and I was responsible? Also I was terrified that if I told anyone we would be taken off Mum and sent to live with Auntie and Uncle again.

So I dealt with it the only way I possibly could. I pretended that it had never happened, tried to forget. But in reality, I never ever forgot. Every day I had Judy there to remind me of what my dad had done. I felt so torn. I wanted to hate her and all that she represented. I didn't want a dog if that was the price that I'd had to pay but I couldn't help but love this bedraggled stray.

Later that day, I went into the kitchen and saw Dad's pound note still on the side. Normally he was taking our money from us rather than giving it to us. So, before I could change my mind, I put it in my pocket and went down to the pet shop in Greenwich and bought Judy a collar and lead.

The next few days were a nightmare. I couldn't bear to be anywhere near my father and if he walked into a room, then I walked out. I was too scared to go to sleep, terrified that he would try and climb into my bed again. I would sit there, wide-awake, with Judy positioned at the top of the ladder so that if I nodded off she would block his way. Dad acted like nothing had happened and it was a relief when, true to form, he went missing again one day. A week later, I was sat up watching telly with Mum one night when he turned up, drunk and abusive.

Now that I was older, I'd started to answer him back and he hated it.

'Go to bed,' he said when he saw me.

'No,' I said. 'I'm not going to bed and leave you to hurt Mum.'

'Shut your fucking mouth, you little c**t, or, I'll belt you,' he slurred.

'Don't you dare touch her,' said Mum.

'I'll show her what happens if she talks back to me,' he said, unravelling his belt from around his suit trousers and lashing out at me with it. I flinched as the buckle end whacked me on the cheekbone.

'I said get to fucking bed,' he roared.

In the end, Mum dragged me to my bedroom.

'Please go to bed or he'll really hurt you,' she pleaded.

The poor woman looked terrified. I knew she'd started to hit rock bottom again. She hadn't said anything but I could tell as she'd been so quiet lately and I'd often find her crying.

The next day, Dad went straight back to the pub again as soon as it opened. All of us kids were in the front room getting ready for bed when he came staggering in.

Him and Mum started to row straight away. I could hear Mum screaming as he walloped her over and over again. Davina put her hands over her ears and Laraine started to cry.

'Come here, Lal,' I said, putting my arms around her. 'It will be OK.'

David and I looked at each other. We'd heard it all before but it was still terrifying.

'Right, that's it,' I heard Mum say. 'I'm leaving, I can't take any more. I'm going to walk out of that door and never come back.'

Panic rose up in my throat.

Please don't go, I thought to myself. Don't leave us with that man.

'If you go then I'll cut your children's throats,' yelled Dad. 'And you'd better fucking believe it.'

Mum obviously did because thankfully it was Dad who stormed out that night, but I knew she had reached the end of her tether. The next day Granddad George came round with his tool bag.

'What are you doing, Granddad?' I asked as he got out a drill.

'I'm changing the locks so that no good father of yours can't get in,' he said.

'Don't worry,' he told Mum. 'That bastard won't be bothering you any more.'

That was fine by me after everything my father had done. I hated him and all I felt was relief as Laraine and I watched Granddad get to work.

'But what about when he comes back?' I asked him. 'He's going to go mental if he can't get in.'

'I've told your mother to phone the police,' said Granddad.

That night, for the first time in four days, I slept. Sure enough, Dad turned up a couple of nights later. Laraine and I were woken up by hammering on the front door of our flat.

'Open this fucking door, you bitch, or I'll kick it in,' he shouted.

'I'm calling the police, Fred,' Mum yelled.

Everything went quiet and ten minutes later there was a knock at the door.

'Open up, it's the police,' said a gruff voice.

Mum opened the door to two officers and they explained that when Dad had seen their panda car pull up, he'd legged it.

'Funnily enough, we need to speak to your husband as he's on suspicion of handling stolen goods, amongst other things,' they said.

Bleary-eyed, we were all dragged out of our beds while officers once again searched our house. This time they came out with a clock and a jewellery box that I'd never seen before.

'If Freddie comes back again tell him we're looking for him,' said an officer. 'He's had enough warnings. I'm afraid this time his luck has run out.'

'Is Dad going to get arrested?' David whispered to me.

'I hope so,' I said.

The news was music to my ears. I still had over five weeks of the summer holidays left and I knew I'd feel much safer if Dad was locked away inside.

It was a relief to have Dad gone but I also knew how hard it was for Mum. To keep food in the cupboards and the rent and bills paid, she needed her cleaning jobs more than ever. She would take Davina with her, leaving Laraine and I in the flat while David went to his friend's house down the road.

Normally we would have played with Peggy and Susan but just before the start of the school holidays, Estelle had come down to tell Mum that they were moving out.

'We're buying a house in Charlton,' she told us. 'It's only down the road and you can come over and see us whenever you want.'

But all of us kids were gutted: visiting wasn't the same as having our best friends upstairs and running in and out of each other's houses. Laraine and I had been in tears the day they'd moved out. So now, with the flat upstairs still empty, there really was no one to play with when Mum went to work.

'You two be good,' she told us as she ran out of the door one morning in the second week of the holidays. 'There's squash and crisps in the cupboard if you get hungry and I'll be back at lunchtime.

'And remember, don't go any further than the front garden.'

Laraine and I played marbles, then hide and seek and tig. The time seemed to drag and we soon got bored. So there was great excitement when we looked out of the window to see a big removal van pull up outside.

'That must be the new people,' I said to Laraine.

Ian and Estelle's flat had been empty for the past couple of weeks and we were desperate to get new neighbours, especially if it meant new kids to play with.

We watched out of the window as the front door was wedged open and two men piled up boxes in the porch. Laraine's big brown eyes lit up when she saw them bring in a pushchair.

'There must be a baby, Deb,' she said. 'I love babies.'

Over the next few days I tried desperately to catch a glimpse of the new people. The back garden belonged to our flat but we always played in the big communal front garden, where we could see who went in and out.

'Well, I met the new lady upstairs today,' Mum told us one night. 'Her name's Wendy and she's got three kids.'

Mum said they weren't from Blackheath, so she'd offered to give Wendy a tour of the local area the following day.

'I thought I'd show her where the shops are and the doctor's surgery so she can try and get her bearings.'

Me and Laraine went out the front to play the next day to find two boys running around. Shayne was seven, like Laraine, and Michael was eight, the same age as David.

'Our sister Alison's just a baby,' said Michael.

'Yeah,' said Shayne. 'She's only three so she ain't allowed to play out like us.'

They seemed like nice lads and we all had a game of hide and seek. A few days later me and Laraine were playing marbles in the porch when I saw a man coming up the path. He had lanky brown hair pulled back into a ponytail and was wearing sunglasses and a scruffy white T-shirt and jeans. I thought it was strange as he was also wearing a leather jacket even though it was a boiling hot summer's day.

'All right,' I said, giving him a nod.

But he just put his head down and grunted as he went past us and through the front door of the upstairs flat.

'That must be Michael and Shayne's dad,' said Laraine.

'He ain't very friendly,' I laughed.

I asked the lads about it a few days later when we were out playing.

'He's not our old man,' said Michael. 'That's Patrick Ryan, our mum's fella.'

'Our dad's coming to take us to the football this weekend,' said Shayne proudly. 'Then we're off to the seaside next week.'

I shuddered, remembering my own father and all of his broken promises. Sure enough a few days later I saw a handsome, dark-haired man walking down the front path, hand in hand with the boys, who both had big beams on their faces. Lucky them to have a dad who cared, I thought.

Occasionally we'd see Pat, as the boys called him, going up and down the path on his way to the shop. He was a scruffy, dirty-looking bloke. Wendy was a pretty woman who dressed nice and was always made-up, so I wouldn't have put the pair of them together.

'I don't know what she's doing with a funny-looking, miserable fella like him,' said Mum. 'He doesn't even say hello.'

One afternoon Laraine and I were playing in the side return at the back of our flat when we heard tapping. We looked up to see a little girl stood there at a window of the upstairs flat. She was a cute little thing, with big dark eyes and long brown hair in ringlet curls.

'That must be Alison, Michael and Shayne's little sister,' I said.

We waved up to her and she smiled and waved back.

'Aw, she's dead sweet, ain't she, Deb?' said Laraine. 'She's like a little doll.'

She stood up on the sill and shouted out of the open window: 'Come and play with me.'

'Oh please, Deb, can I?' begged Laraine.

I knew how much she loved babies and toddlers. We'd always been in and out of Ian and Estelle's when they lived up there, but Mum had told us not to go out of the flat.

'Please can I go upstairs and say hello to Alison?' she said.

'OK,' I sighed. 'But don't be long.'

'Thanks, Deb,' she said, skipping off inside.

I was conscious that I was the eldest and in charge. Even though David was out playing he was at someone else's house and it had all been arranged. But I needn't have worried. Half an hour later Laraine was back.

'She's a sweet little thing,' she said. 'And she's got loads of Sindy dolls.

'Her mum was at work but that fella Pat was there. He made us some squash and gave us some biscuits.'

It sounded like she'd had a great time.

'Can I go and play tomorrow?' she asked.

'We'll see,' I said. 'But don't tell Mum. She might be cross with me for letting you go up there on your own.'

'Thanks, Deb,' she smiled.

Laraine couldn't wait to go up there again. If only I had known then what was going to happen, I would have stopped her. Then the nightmare might never have begun.

Chapter 5

An Horrific Discovery

A couple of days later, we saw Alison in her bedroom again. She was standing on the windowsill, banging on the window pane. Laraine waved up to her.

'Come and play,' she shouted, pressing one of her Sindy dolls up to the glass.

Laraine looked at me with big pleading eyes.

'Please, Deb,' she begged. 'Can I go?'

I didn't want to spend the summer holidays hanging around with a three-year-old but I knew Laraine didn't have any friends locally like me because her school was so far away. She seemed to be really taken with Alison and as she was quite babyish herself, she always got on better with younger kids rather than girls her own age. I felt a bit mean saying no.

'OK then,' I said. 'But don't be long. Mum will kill me if she knows I've let you out of my sight.'

Like last time, the front door to the upstairs flat was open and I watched Laraine head up the stairs. I went back into our flat and decided to read an Enid Blyton book but I was all fidgety. Mum was out cleaning and had taken Davina with her as usual, and David was playing at his friend Peter's house across the road. Without Laraine to mess around with, it was even more boring being stuck in an empty flat. This summer Mum had told me that I was finally old enough to be allowed to go to the local park on my own. It was only a little playground, about a fifteen-minute walk away, but it felt like such a big deal. I knew Mum had probably meant I could go when she was around, but Judy needed a walk so I decided to take her down there.

It was a lovely sunny morning, too nice to be cooped up inside, and I felt so grown up as I strode down the hill on my own. But as soon as I got there, I suddenly felt guilty.

What if Laraine came back down and I wasn't there and she panicked or got upset? I was cross with myself for not shouting upstairs and letting her know I was going out. I knew Mum would be furious with me if she found out that I'd left her.

'Sorry, girl,' I said, pulling Judy's lead. 'We're going to have to go home.'

I hurried back as quickly as I could; it was boiling hot and I was sweating as I dragged Judy up the hill towards the flat.

It's OK, I told myself. Everything will be fine.

But it wasn't. As I walked into the porch and pushed open the heavy front entrance door, I heard it. It was a sound that made me stop dead in my tracks.

Screaming.

I knew instantly who it was.

'Laraine?' I shouted. 'Where are you? Don't worry, I'm here, Lal.'

I could tell that it was coming from upstairs. In a complete panic, I quickly opened the front door of our flat and pushed Judy inside. My heart was pounding as I pulled open the unlocked front door of Alison's flat and ran up the steep flight of stairs. As I was halfway up, I was confronted with the most horrific sight. Lying on the landing floor was my terrified sister and on top of her was Patrick Ryan. Her shorts were pulled down around her knees and she was crying. I couldn't see what he was doing to her but his jeans were down and even though I was only nine, because of everything that had happened with my father I knew instantly that it was wrong.

'Don't you dare touch my sister,' I screamed, jumping on his back. 'Get away from her.'

I grabbed his greasy ponytail and tried to pull him off her.

Pat looked shocked to see me and he tried to get up off Laraine, who was sobbing now. In the scuffle to get him off her, I don't know what happened. Suddenly I heard a scream and to my horror, Laraine tumbled head first down the stairs. She landed at the bottom with a bang and for a second everything went quiet.

That's it, I thought. She's dead.

I was so shocked, I couldn't move. I just stared at her

curled up in a ball at the bottom of the stairs. It was such a relief when she started whimpering.

Pat didn't say a word; he just stood there and pulled his jeans up while I ran down the stairs to my little sister.

Blood was streaming down Laraine's face and I could see that she'd got a cut above her right eye. Her National Health glasses that we both wore had snapped at the side. I helped her off the floor and pulled up her shorts.

'Don't worry, Lal, you're safe now,' I told her. 'I'll get you home.'

Leaning on me for support, she hobbled into our flat and I locked the door behind us. I took her into the bathroom, closed the lid of the toilet and sat her down on it. It was like I was on autopilot and neither of us said anything. Laraine was in shock. She was shaking and she couldn't speak; she could barely even cry.

I filled the sink with hot water and Dettol and wrung out a flannel. As gently as I could, I bathed her eye. To me being abused was becoming frighteningly normal. Was this what all men did?

But not to my little sister, no one was going to touch my poor Lal. She was seven years old for God's sake, a tiny, fragile girl. Thank goodness I had come back to the flat when I did and interrupted them.

I looked at the clock: we didn't have long. It was 1.30pm and Mum was due back from work soon. I finished cleaning Laraine's eye and fixed her glasses by wrapping plasters around the broken arm. Laraine and

I never talked about it but I knew I couldn't tell Mum what had happened. I was worried that she would be cross with me if she found out that I had gone out and left Laraine in the flats on her own. I was also still terrified that if I told her, Social Services would blame Mum and we would all be put back into care again. No, we had no choice, our lips would have to stay sealed.

A few minutes later Mum came in through the door, pushing Davina. When I saw her face, it took all my strength not to burst into tears and tell her what that nasty man upstairs had done to Laraine but I knew I couldn't.

'What happened?' she said when she saw Laraine's cut and patched-up glasses.

'Lal fell over in the garden and broke her specs, but it ain't her fault,' I told her.

Laraine still looked completely shell-shocked and didn't say anything.

'Aw, my poor little love,' said Mum, going over to her and giving her a hug. 'Have you been crying? Don't look so worried, it doesn't matter. I'll get you a plaster for your head.'

Laraine hardly said a word for the rest of the day, she just seemed to be in a daze. We hadn't talked about what had happened but I knew I had to say something. That night we lay in our bunk beds in the dark, neither of us asleep. Every time I closed my eyes I just kept seeing that disgusting man on top of my little sister.

'Lal?' I whispered.

'Yes, Deb.'

'Please don't ever go upstairs to that flat again.'

There was a pause.

'But Deb, Alison's my friend,' she said.

The thought of ever stepping foot in that flat again and seeing him made me shudder but Laraine seemed determined. It's hard to understand and I know what you're thinking. Why would we go up there when we knew what he was capable of? Why would we go back again if we were so terrified of him?

But the truth is, I don't really know. All I can say is that we were seven and nine, we were children. Alison was Laraine's little friend, her only friend. She was too young to understand what was happening to her. In her innocent mind, all she wanted was someone to play with.

But I knew it was wrong and I couldn't bear the thought of him hurting my little sister. If Laraine was going to go up there again, I was going to have to go with her. As far as I was concerned, that monster was never going to be given the opportunity to abuse her again.

* * *

Days went by and I tried to get any thoughts about Patrick Ryan out of my head.

A week later Laraine and I were messing about in the porch, playing marbles. As usual, Mum was out cleaning and David was at a friend's house. Suddenly we heard a voice coming from upstairs. The flat door was open and there was Alison, sitting on the top step.

'Hi Laraine,' she said. 'Are you coming up to play with me?'

Laraine looked at me but she knew exactly what I was going to say.

'No way,' I whispered to her.

'Ple-e-e-ase,' begged Alison. 'Come and see my Sindy dolls, Laraine.'

I felt sick at the thought of either of us being anywhere near Patrick Ryan but I knew I couldn't stop Laraine. With or without my blessing, she was going to go up there and there was no way on this earth I was going to let her go up there alone.

'If you're gonna go up there then I'm coming with you,' I told her.

We went upstairs and followed Alison into the front room. Their flat was a lot nicer than ours. The walls were all freshly painted and the furniture was newer. I couldn't see Pat but I could hear him banging about in the kitchen.

I was on edge knowing that he was in the house. I sat on the sofa while the girls played with some dolls on the floor. Eventually Pat came in. He didn't say a word to me or Laraine, didn't even look at us.

'Alison get to your room, it's nap time,' he said to her.

She did as he said straight away.

'Bye, Laraine,' she called, giving her a wave as Pat took her to her bedroom.

'Right, we're going,' I whispered to Laraine, getting up to leave.

But before she could reply, Pat came back into the room.

'Get Alison a drink, will you,' he said to me. 'There's some squash in the kitchen.'

I didn't want to leave Laraine but I was so terrified of him, I did what he said. Besides, I knew he wouldn't dare touch her if I was around.

I went to the kitchen, which was down a little flight of stairs at the back of the house, just like ours. On the side were some pink beakers. I didn't know where anything was so I hunted round for ages until I found a bottle of orange squash in one of the cupboards and poured it out. I thought I'd better take the beaker of juice back to Pat so I carried it carefully into the living room. As I walked in the door, I gasped. Patrick Ryan was on top of my sister on the floor, abusing her again.

I dropped the squash onto the floor and it went all over the grey cord carpet.

'Get off her,' I screamed, running towards him.

And just like before, I tried to pull him off Laraine. She wasn't screaming or crying like last time. She just lay there motionless on the floor, her eyes closed like she was in some sort of a trance.

'I said get off her,' I screamed, pulling at his dirty white T-shirt.

'You leave my sister alone or I'm going to tell my mum about you.'

'No, you're not,' he spat, 'My brother's a policeman and no one will believe you.'

'And if you do,' he said, coming so close to me I could smell the stale beer on his breath. 'I'll kill you both and your mum.'

I was shaking, completely terrified. I believed every word of it.

Meanwhile, Laraine was still lying there motionless. Even when I helped her off the floor and pulled her shorts up, she showed no reaction.

'Lal, you're OK,' I said. 'Talk to me,'

But she didn't say a word and just stared straight ahead into space.

As I helped her out, Pat was stood by the door.

'Why are you doing this to her?' I said. 'Why can't you just leave her alone?'

An evil grin spread across his face.

'There's only one way of making sure that I'll leave her alone,' he sneered. 'And that's if you let me do it to you.'

'You're never touching her again,' I said.

'Only if you let me touch you instead,' he replied.

I was so horrified, I didn't say a word. I helped Laraine down the stairs to our flat.

When I closed the front door, I was shaking like a leaf. I was absolutely terrified of Patrick Ryan. What kind of animal would dare do that to a seven-year-old girl?

I knew I couldn't let that happen to Laraine again. When Mum and Davina came back a few hours later, I never mentioned a thing. I didn't dare now that he'd threatened to kill us. I believed everything he'd said and I knew he meant every word.

Over the next few days neither of us talked about what had happened but I could see the effect it had had on Laraine. She insisted on sleeping with the light on and one night she shook me awake.

'Deb,' she whispered. 'I've had an accident.'

The poor thing had wet the bed and she was devastated.

'It's OK, Lal, it doesn't matter,' I reassured her. 'We'll wash your sheets out tomorrow when Mum's at work and put them out in the garden to dry. She'll never know.'

'Come and get in with me.'

'Thank you, Deb,' she said.

She climbed up to the top bunk and snuggled into me. As I cuddled up against her frail little body, I knew whatever happened I couldn't let Patrick Ryan hurt her again. She was my little sister, it was my job to protect her. No, I would never let him touch her again. But I knew there was only one way Patrick Ryan would agree to that. The thought of it made me feel sick but if it was either me or Laraine, I knew what I had to do: I would have to sacrifice myself to save my sister.

Chapter 6

The Ultimate Sacrifice

I didn't have to wait long until our next run-in with Patrick Ryan. Three days, in fact.

I was playing in the garden with Judy one afternoon when I realised that I hadn't seen Laraine for a while.

'Lal?' I shouted in the back door. 'Lal, where are you?'

As soon as I set foot inside our flat, I knew instantly where she'd gone. My stomach was churning with dread as I walked out of our front door and up the stairs to the flat above. I tried to prepare myself for what I was going to find this time. Whenever I closed my eyes, I'd see an image of Patrick Ryan on top of my poor little sister and that awful distant look on her face. To my surprise, there was no one on the landing but I could hear noises coming from the kitchen.

Oh God, had he got her in there?

I ran in, expecting the worst, but Pat was there on his own.

'Where's my sister?' I said. 'I've come to get her.'

'She's playing with Alison in the front room,' he said gruffly.

After everything that had happened I still didn't believe he hadn't touched her. I ran up the small flight of stairs into the front room and there were Laraine and Alison sitting on the floor, eating sweets out of Russian dolls.

'Look what Pat gave us, Deb,' said Laraine, lifting hers up and showing me some pink Jelly Tots stuffed inside.

I was relieved that she was OK but cross with her at the same time.

'I told you not to come up here without me,' I said.

'When I went inside for a wee I heard Alison calling me,' she replied.

I was angry and annoyed that she still wanted to go up there after everything that had happened. I didn't want to be anywhere near that man, especially after what he'd said to me last time about only leaving Laraine alone if he could abuse me instead. Pat had come back into the front room.

'I'm thirsty,' said Alison. 'Please can I have some juice?'

'I'll go and get you some from the kitchen,' he said.

He came back in with two pink beakers of orange squash and handed them to Alison and Laraine.

'I'll go and get mine,' I said.

In hindsight I shouldn't have left the safety of the living room but I didn't think. Instead, I walked straight into his trap.

I was getting my drink when Pat came back into the kitchen. I picked up my beaker but as I turned around to walk out of the door, I felt his arm around my neck, dragging me back. I was so shocked, I dropped the cup and juice splashed all over the floor.

My hands were shaking and I was rooted to the spot. You see I knew instinctively that he was going to abuse me. Pat pulled me up the stairs that led down to the kitchen and took me onto the landing. I desperately wanted to fight back but I knew it was hopeless. Even though I was a chubby nine-year-old and not a skinny little thing like Laraine, I stood no chance against a fully-grown man. Patrick Ryan wasn't muscly like my dad but he was tall, and to me he seemed huge. He pushed me onto the floor.

'What are you doing?' I whimpered.

I soon found out what horror he had in store. He pulled his jeans down and forced his willy into my mouth. Holding the back of my head, he moved me backwards and forwards on him again and again. It was horrible. I couldn't move or breathe and I really thought I was going to choke.

It only lasted a couple of minutes until a gloopy, salty liquid gushed into my mouth and hit the back of my throat. It was so disgusting that I retched and was violently sick. He was fuming.

'You stupid little bitch,' he said, hitting me round the side of my head.

I felt so humiliated. I was nine years old and being made to do this to this man. The kind of thing you only do when you're intimate with someone as an adult. Not to a scared, bewildered child.

He handed me a pink tissue and I wiped my mouth and my face and then without saying a word, he went back to the front room. I ran downstairs to the safety of our flat and locked myself in the bathroom. My face ached and my throat burned. I couldn't stop thinking about what Patrick Ryan had done to me and I was violently sick again. I swilled my mouth out with TCP but I was convinced I could still taste that disgusting white goo, so I got the bottle of Dettol and took a big sip. For a split second I considered swallowing it but it burnt me so badly that I spat it out. My lips and the inside of my mouth were smarting but I didn't care. Any pain was better than the taste of him.

Half an hour later, Mum and Davina came back. It was hard acting normal and pretending that nothing had happened. I didn't dare say a word as I knew what Patrick Ryan would do to my family if I told.

I was desperate to get out of the flat and try and clear my head.

'I'm gonna take Judy to the park,' I told Mum.

'OK,' she said. 'But please be careful, mind the roads and don't be long.'

I walked to the little park down the hill and when I got there, I took off Judy's collar and lead and let her have a run. I sat on the swing and watched her chasing around, sniffing trees and pawing at sticks. I thought of everything that had happened to me in those past two weeks and I felt sick. First my dad, then Laraine being abused by Patrick Ryan and now me. Why were these awful things happening? Why me? Was it something that I'd done? Was it my fault?

It had all started with my father and that silly, scraggy old mutt. Even though I loved Judy with all my heart, I didn't want to. As I watched her running around the park I realised that every day I looked at her she would just be a constant reminder of this horrendous summer and how dirty and disgusting I felt.

So I did something terrible, something even now I'm so ashamed of. I got up, threw Judy's collar and lead in the bin and walked away.

'I'm sorry, Judy,' I whispered to myself as I headed home without her. 'I can't love you any more.'

She had become a symbol of every bad thing that had happened to me and I didn't want her. But I still cried my heart out as I walked home up the hill.

'Where's the dog?' asked Mum when I got back.

'She ran off again,' I lied. 'I've looked everywhere.'

'Don't worry, love, I bet she'll turn up,' she said.

Judy had managed to get out of the garden a couple of times and had always come home a few days later. But this time I knew it was different. She'd never find her way back from the park.

I felt so guilty that night I couldn't sleep.

Please let somebody find her and look after her, I told myself.

Busy Greenwich High Street was only a few second's

walk from the park and I was worried that she might have got run over. Even though I didn't want her, I didn't want anything bad to happen to her and I hoped someone nice would take her in.

The next morning Mum came rushing into mine and Laraine's bedroom.

'Guess who's home?' she smiled.

The next minute I heard a bark and Judy came padding in.

'Judy!' said Laraine. 'She's back.'

I was so relieved to see her and that she was OK, I burst into tears.

'I'm so sorry, girl,' I whispered.

No matter how hard I tried or what she reminded me of, I couldn't stop myself from loving her.

I had prayed that it was a one-off but over the next few weeks Patrick Ryan continued to abuse me. Every morning I would wake up and think, 'Is he going to hurt me today?'

He would take his chance whenever Laraine went up to play with Alison and I would follow as there was no way I wanted her to be alone in that flat.

One afternoon he dragged me out of the kitchen and pushed me onto the landing. To my horror, he started to perform oral sex on me. I didn't know what it was called at the time but I knew it was horrible and I felt so embarrassed having to lie there while he put his tongue inside me. It really hurt my legs, and my thighs were red raw where his stubble rubbed my skin but it was more the humiliation of having to lie there while he did these things to me that I hated.

Another time he pulled down my shorts then he went off to the bathroom and came back with a pink bottle. I knew it was bubble bath as it was similar to the ones that my mum ordered from the Avon catalogue. As he poured some of the gloopy pink liquid on his fingers, the strong flowery smell almost made me gag. I felt sick with fear, wondering what he was going to do next. I soon found out. Pain seared through my body as he rammed his fingers deep inside me.

I shut my eyes and tried not to cry. I told myself, please don't let Laraine come out of the living room and find me like this.

But another part of me was hoping that someone did walk up the stairs. I didn't want to tell anybody but I wanted somebody to catch him, to find out what he was doing to me. I constantly begged and pleaded with Laraine not to go anywhere near the upstairs flat.

'I don't want to go up there,' I would tell her. 'I can't face it.'

But no matter what I said, as soon as she heard Alison calling her she would go up there regardless. One morning I realised that she had gone up there without even asking me. As soon as I realised that she had gone, I was up there like a shot. Whatever happened I wasn't going to let my sister be up there on her own. The flat door was open as always and as I bolted up the stairs, I saw Patrick Ryan on the landing.

'Come to find your sister, have you?' he said. 'I was just about to go and get her from the front room.'

'No!' I said. 'You're not going to touch her again. I'm going to take her home right now.'

I marched towards the front room but before I could go any further, he grabbed me and threw me down onto the landing floor.

I was frozen with fear as he pulled down my shorts and pants, then he stood over me and started to unbuckle his belt and unzip the flies of his dirty jeans.

Please God, no, don't let him do this.

He didn't say a word but I knew what was about to happen. With his trousers around his ankles, he lunged towards me. He still had on the same grubby white T-shirt that he always wore and the smell of sweat was so strong it made me gag.

He stared at me with such a look of disgust, like I was something he'd trodden on in the street. I'll never forget his horrible face with his lanky brown hair scraped back in a ponytail and that dodgy left eye that turned inwards and never moved. I closed my own eyes because I couldn't bear to look at him.

I could hear Alison and Laraine chatting as they played in the front room. Too far away for them to hear or see anything.

At least it's not Laraine, I told myself. This is what I had to do to protect her.

'Open your eyes,' he ordered as he climbed on top of me and forced my legs apart.

'I don't want to,' I mumbled.

'I said open your fucking eyes,' he sneered.

I did as he said because I was so terrified, but I didn't want to see what was happening. I just wanted to transport my mind far, far away and pray this would be over and done with as quickly as possible.

As he lay down on top of me, I felt like I'd been winded. I couldn't breathe, I couldn't move. The back of his hand was holding my hair down on the carpet so I couldn't lift my head up. He tried to kiss me but I clamped my mouth shut. So he squeezed both my cheeks until my lips gaped open like a fish then he forced his tongue in. It was disgusting and the taste of cigarettes and stale beer made me retch.

As he forced himself inside me, an excruciating, burning pain seared through me and it felt like my body was being ripped in two. I could feel the rough grey cord carpet underneath me rubbing the backs of my legs and bottom red raw like sandpaper.

But I didn't cry. I just told myself over and over again: This is what you have to do to stop him hurting Laraine.

It seemed to go on forever until suddenly I felt a wet sensation between my legs and Pat jumped up.

'Oh, for fuck's sake, you've gone and pissed yourself,' he said.

I felt so ashamed.

'I-I'm sorry,' I stuttered. 'I didn't mean to.'

He was so angry he hit me round the side of the head.

'You dirty little c**t,' he growled.

He held out his penis and urinated all over me.

It was the ultimate humiliation and I felt so dirty. Somehow him weeing on me was almost worse than the actual rape itself.

He pulled up his trousers and handed me some pink tissues.

'Clean yourself up,' he said.

He stood there watching while I wiped myself between my legs. It really stung and I could see that I was bleeding.

'Now get your fucking clothes back on,' he said, giving me a look of utter disgust.

My legs were all wobbly and I felt like I might pass out but I did as he said. As quickly as I could, I pulled up my pants and shorts and in a daze followed him into the front room.

The girls were still stuffing their faces with Jelly Tots, oblivious to the horror that had been going on outside on the landing. Alison had the little Russian doll, Laraine had the middle-sized one and now Pat held out the biggest doll to me.

I shook my head – I didn't want anything from him.

'We've got to go home now,' I said. 'Come on, Laraine.'

Laraine and I went downstairs in silence. If we spoke, I was afraid that I would cry and then she'd ask me what had happened. I didn't ever want her to know what I'd had to do to keep her safe.

'What time is it?' said Laraine. 'Will Mummy be home soon?'

I looked at the clock and said, 'Yes, Lal, she will.'

I knew I didn't have long. I went into the bathroom and locked the door. We only ever had a bath once a week on a Sunday but I desperately needed to have a wash and to try and get the smell and the taste of that disgusting man off me.

I knew the drill by now. It was in here that I'd washed myself after my father had raped me and cleaned myself up after Patrick Ryan had forced me to give him oral sex. I swilled my mouth out with TCP, then I got the Dettol. I felt so dirty, I didn't even bother to dilute it. I just tipped it onto a flannel neat and scrubbed myself all over.

My skin burned from the disinfectant but I didn't mind. It gave me a different kind of pain to focus on and the stinging sensation made me feel better. At least there wasn't as much blood this time. My father had already paved the way for that monster but there was still a bit soaked into my pants. So I changed my shorts and underwear and buried my blood-stained knickers at the bottom of the kitchen bin so Mum couldn't find them.

When Mum came home I was scared that she was going to be able to tell what had happened. I was so sore down below, I could barely walk, and my cheeks and chin were raw and painful from where his stubbly face had rubbed against me. But she didn't say anything and I was too terrified to tell her, of course.

At least the one place that I did feel safe was our flat. Unlike the time my father had raped me, when the front door was closed I knew Patrick Ryan couldn't get anywhere near me. It was a small comfort but at least it was something. That was until I heard Mum tutting in her bedroom one morning.

'That man is disgusting,' she said.

'What man?' I asked.

'That bloke Pat from upstairs.'

Just the mention of his name made me flinch.

'Why?' I asked, trying to sound casual. 'What's he done?'

'The dirty pig has been weeing out of his bedroom window in the night. It reeks out here.'

Pat and Wendy's bedroom window was at the side of the house above my mum's. You could see the pool of yellow liquid on her windowsill and there was no mistaking that pungent smell on a hot summer's morning.

'Honestly, the man's an animal. I don't know why he can't use a toilet like normal people.'

Because he'd urinated on me after he'd raped me, I felt like it was a message for me. A little reminder from him that he was there, watching me.

Sometimes he'd bang on our door late at night when he came in from the pub. I'd be asleep but Judy would be lying next to me on the top bunk and she'd start barking and I'd wake up in a panic. I knew it was him because afterwards I'd hear the door to the upstairs flat slam shut; the hairs on the back of my neck would stand up in fear as I heard the heavy tread of his footsteps on the stairs. Even in my own home, he wouldn't let me forget that he was still around, waiting for the next chance he got to pounce on me.

Chapter 7

Broken Promises

Patrick Ryan wasn't always so clever. Laraine had sneaked up there one afternoon and as usual, I'd come to find her straight away. Her and Alison were playing dolls on the landing and he was lurking around them, which always made me nervous.

'Go get the cups from the front room and tidy up these toys because Mum's going to be home soon,' he told Alison.

The pair of them trotted off to do what he'd asked and I followed them. That was until I felt a hand grip my arm.

'Where do you think you're going?' he said. 'Get in here.'

Dragging me by my hair, he pulled me into one of the bedrooms, which I realised was Shayne and Michael's. They had bunk beds like me and Laraine, and the floor was covered with Tonka toys and Matchbox cars. He pushed me onto the carpet next to a mini snooker table and pulled down his jeans and grubby white Y-fronts. I closed my eyes and steeled myself for what was about to happen when suddenly, outside the door, I heard Alison's voice.

'Michael, Shayne, what are you doing back? Debbie and Laraine are here.'

Panic shot across Pat's face. For a second he froze like a rabbit caught in the headlights, then he jumped up off me and pulled his trousers up. Without saying a word, he stood up and walked out.

'Hello, lads,' I heard him say. 'You're back early.'

I was relieved that I hadn't been put through my usual ordeal but I was a bit shaken too. I got up and went out onto the landing.

'All right,' I said. 'I was just having a look at your toys.'

I was so relieved the boys hadn't walked in and seen what he was doing. I would have been so ashamed if they'd found me like that.

That was the one and only occasion I saw Patrick Ryan lose his cool.

Over the summer the abuse continued. It didn't happen every time we went up there – sometimes Michael and Shayne would be due back from their dad's and we were never ever there when Wendy was around. As soon as she came home, the front door was closed and locked.

Patrick Ryan was clever. He always raped me on the landing in exactly the same position with him facing the front door so he could see if anyone was coming up the stairs. He would attack me while the girls were playing and eating sweets in the front room. Laraine would never question where I'd been. In fact I don't think it ever even entered her mind.

He would say, 'Can you go and get some sweets or a drink for the children?' Then he would follow me into the kitchen.

I always knew what was going to happen but I still went. I suppose I was deliberately putting myself in those situations so that he wouldn't touch Laraine. It didn't really matter if I was used and abused. After all, I was already damaged goods after what the foster parents and my father had done to me.

It wasn't easy though, and I felt sick a lot of the time, knowing what was to come. Part of me just switched off and I tried to stop myself from thinking or feeling anything. It was the only way that I could get through it.

I became resigned to the fact that this was what I had to do in order to stop him hurting my little sister. I was sacrificing myself to protect Laraine and that thought was the only thing that kept me going.

I quickly learned to lie there and do nothing while Pat was raping me. He hated it when I showed no reaction. The more I moved and struggled, the more that animal seemed to enjoy it and the more it hurt. If I just lay there then it would all be over quite quickly. Afterwards he would always hand me some pink tissues from the bathroom to clean myself up. Then he would take me back into the front room where the girls were and I'd have to act like there was nothing wrong. I had always dreaded the long summer holidays but this was living hell. The only thing that kept me going was the thought that they would eventually end. The days seemed to be dragging so slowly and, unlike every other kid, going back to school couldn't come quickly enough for me. As the end of the holidays drew near, I was getting braver.

One day after he'd raped me he whispered in my ear, 'You're the best little fuck I've ever had.'

But I'd had enough of being used and abused.

'Well, I don't want to be,' I told him defiantly.

I could see he was shocked and annoyed that I'd answered him back.

'I'll show you what you get for mouthing off at me,' he said, pushing me back down onto the floor and performing oral sex on me.

Afterwards he forced me down onto my knees and pushed his penis into my mouth. I gagged at the taste and smell of stale wee and it took all my willpower not to be sick.

'That will fucking teach you not to answer me back again,' he hissed, his face twisted with hate.

For the first time I couldn't stop myself from crying. I had tried so hard to not feel anything, to switch off when he was doing these awful things to me but this was too much.

'Why do you keep doing this to me?' I sobbed. 'Why do you keep hurting me?'

He smiled.

'If I wasn't doing it to you then I'd be doing it to your sister,' he said. 'And the only difference between you and her is that she don't piss herself.'

I went home that day and threw up again and again, until my stomach was empty, but I was still too scared to tell a soul. I was ashamed and embarrassed to describe these awful things that were happening to me. Maybe if someone had asked, I would have told. But nobody ever did and so it became my secret. The secret that I had to keep to save my sister. I couldn't confide in Laraine because I was doing all of this to protect her. She'd already been abused by that monster, that was enough for any seven-year-old, and she was still messing herself and having nightmares. No, this was something I had to learn to live with and keep to myself.

As if things couldn't get any worse in my life, Mum got a letter.

'It's from your dad,' she told us all. 'He's in prison.'

We hadn't heard anything from him during the five weeks since he'd turned up and tried to get into the flat after Granddad had changed the locks. The police had eventually caught up with him and arrested and charged him: he'd been convicted of handling stolen goods, drink driving and driving without a licence.

'He's in Lewes prison,' said Mum. 'He says he loves and misses us all and he wants us to go and see him. He's sent us some visiting orders.'

I couldn't believe what I was hearing. After everything

Dad had done to our family and to me, I never wanted to be in the same room as him again. It had been a relief not to have him in our lives any more. I was angry that Mum would want anything to do with him after how badly he'd treated her.

'I ain't going,' I told her. 'I hate him.'

'But he's your father,' said Mum. 'He's not allowed to drink in prison and he says he's changed. We can't just leave him there and not go and see him.'

'I don't care, I'm not going,' I said. 'As far as I'm concerned, he can stay in there and rot.'

But Mum refused to leave me at home all day on my own, so I had to go. All of us got the train there and I felt sick the whole of the hour-long journey. Davina was too little to know how she felt and David and Laraine were just desperate to have a dad in their lives, no matter what he'd done. I was dreading seeing him, and I could see Mum was anxious too.

We were taken into a visitor's room, where Dad was waiting in a blue jumpsuit. I was hoping that he would be behind a big plastic screen like you see in the films but he was sat on a normal chair, which meant that unfortunately he was able to kiss and cuddle us. I hung back with Mum while the others rushed over to him.

'Hello, Princess,' he said to me. 'Come and sit on my lap.'

I shook my head, I couldn't even look at him.

'Come and sit with Daddy, Deb,' said Laraine, clambering onto his knee.

I didn't want him to get angry, but I felt so uncomfortable. I couldn't bear to be anywhere near him after what he'd done to me.

'Hello, Mo,' he said to Mum, giving her a peck on the cheek, but I could tell that she was wary of him too.

As Dad wasn't allowed to drink in prison, he'd been sober for weeks and was very charming and full of stories about what life was like behind bars.

'We have to do chores in here to earn some cash, but instead of spending it on fags like all the other lads, I bought some sweets for my beautiful kids,' he said proudly, showing us a packet of Fruit Pastilles.

He made such a big deal out of what a kind, generous father he was.

'This is for being a good girl, Debbie, and for helping your mum while I've been banged up,' he said, handing me a sweet.

I pushed his hand away.

'No thanks,' I said.

I couldn't cope with another man trying to give me sweets after he'd abused me, trying to buy my silence with one measly Fruit Pastille.

I felt so relieved when visiting time was over and I walked out of that prison into the fresh air. Dad sent us visiting orders every six to eight weeks but because it was a long way and the train fare was expensive, thankfully we didn't go again.

He would still write to Mum every week. I always

knew it was him because he had really lovely neat handwriting that you wouldn't expect from such a nasty, violent man. I sneaked a look at them occasionally and they'd be all about how much he loved Mum and us kids, and wanted to make a fresh start when he was released. I was terrified that she would eventually take him back and he would come and live with us again.

Finally, something good happened in my life. The summer holidays ended and I practically ran back to school. It was such a relief as I knew there was no way Patrick Ryan could get to me as often. Unfortunately, the abuse didn't stop completely, though. Sometimes on the odd time Mum was out working late and Michael and Shayne were at their dad's, Laraine would go upstairs after school and play with Alison. Of course I would follow and Patrick Ryan was there, watching, waiting for his chance to pounce on me.

We'd only been back at school for a week when I came home one night to find Mum in tears. For one horrible second I was worried that Dad was back or she'd found out about Patrick Ryan.

'What is it?' I asked. 'What's happened?'

'Your Granddad George has died,' she sobbed.

He'd been on holiday in Margate with some friends from his sheltered accommodation when he'd had a massive heart attack. He'd collapsed and died on the spot.

The whole family was devastated. Laraine, David and Davina were all close to Granddad, too.

'I can't believe we'll never see him again, Deb,' cried Laraine that night.

I knew there was nothing I could say to make her feel better and we both sobbed ourselves to sleep.

He was buried a few days later but Mum thought it would be too upsetting for us kids to go to the funeral, so we just went to school as normal.

I was absolutely gutted. Granddad was the one and only man in the world that I loved and trusted. He was the one constant in our lives and I knew he would have done anything to protect us. Sometimes when I was being abused, I would daydream that Granddad was on his way round and he would find us. I knew he would never let that happen to me again and he would kill Patrick Ryan with his bare hands. But now he was dead and he wasn't going to save me. No one was.

I just felt well and truly trapped.

Chapter 8

A Ticking Time Bomb

Laraine skipped around the front room in her new dress.

'I love it!' she grinned, twirling around. 'Thank you, Auntie Cecily.'

'Try yours on, Debbie,' said Mum, but I just scowled.

Mum's friend Cecily had come to visit and brought the pair of us matching long, frilly pink dresses to wear to a Christmas party. I hated pink more than anything because of Patrick Ryan's obsession with it. Everything I associated with him was that colour: from the beakers of juice he gave us to the bubble bath that he put on his fingers before he abused me and the tissues he gave me to clean myself up with after he'd raped me.

'I don't like it,' I said. 'I won't wear it.'

'Don't be so ungrateful, just try it on,' said Mum, forcing it over my head.

I wouldn't even look at myself in the mirror.

'You look really pretty,' said Mum. 'Doesn't she, Laraine?'

'It's lovely, Deb, just like a princess,' she smiled.

But I didn't want to look pretty or lovely; I wanted to

look horrible and ugly. I wanted to wear plain clothes so nobody would look twice at me and people would leave me well alone.

It had been nearly sixteen months now since Patrick Ryan had started abusing me. What had happened first with my dad and then him had changed me. I knew I wasn't the same little girl who had left school on the first day of the summer holidays that sunny July afternoon.

I'd started to hate myself and I wouldn't look in the mirror any more. When I got dressed of a morning I deliberately chose clothes that I knew would be tricky for Patrick Ryan to take off. It was a relief when summer was over and Mum stopped making me wear dresses, shorts and skirts. Now I always made a point of only wearing trousers and with zips, buckles and buttons rather than elasticated waists. Anything in fact to make it more difficult for that monster upstairs.

I couldn't bear anyone touching me these days either. For weeks my right ear had been aching but I didn't dare tell Mum because I knew she would insist on taking me to the doctor's. But I didn't want anyone, even a lady GP, poking, prodding and examining me, so I kept quiet. Even when watery yellow liquid came oozing out of it onto my pillow and I couldn't sleep because I was in agony, I never said a thing until Mum noticed my ear was bright red.

'You're burning up, young lady, and there's all sorts of gunk in your ear,' she said. 'You've got an infection.'

'I don't care,' I said. 'Leave me alone. I'm not going to see no doctor.'

Mum couldn't understand what was happening to me.

'You used to be such a sweet little thing,' she said. 'Now you're just so angry all the time.'

She was right, I *was* angry. Angry at the world, at everyone. I was like a ticking time bomb just waiting to go off – and occasionally I did. Like the time at school when I was walking down the corridor and a lad I knew tapped me on the shoulder as I walked past.

'Alright, speccy four-eyes,' he said.

Kids often called me that because of the horrible brown National Health glasses that I wore. It was just a silly remark, and me and my mates were always trading insults. It would never have bothered me before and I would have laughed it off, but now I was like a tightly coiled spring and I just snapped.

'What did you say?' I shouted, walking back over to him.

'Nothing,' he said, looking terrified. 'I was just joking.'

'Nobody calls me names,' I said, punching him hard in the face.

Blood pumped out of his nose and he started crying. A teacher had witnessed what had happened and I was marched off to see Mr Matthews, the head teacher.

'Debbie, why on earth have you been fighting?' he asked me. 'It's not like you. You've always been such a well-behaved pupil.'

I shrugged my shoulders.

'You're a conscientious student and I don't ever want to see you acting like that again. Do you understand?'

'Yes, sir,' I mumbled.

I knew I was lucky to escape with a week of detentions.

I didn't want to mess school up as it was the one thing in my life that I enjoyed. I loved English lessons and PE and I even liked getting homework as it kept me busy at night and gave me something to take my mind off the fact that Patrick Ryan was walking around upstairs above us.

I didn't like the person I had become but I couldn't stop myself. I was aggressive, nasty and argumentative. Something else had changed too – I'd started to resent Laraine. It had always been my job to protect her but I began to tell myself it was because of her all this was going on, so I started to blame her. If she'd never gone up there in the first place, none of this would have happened. I knew she had been hurt and abused by Patrick Ryan too and it had always been this unspoken bond between us. But as we got older, instead of bringing us closer together, it wedged us further apart.

I'd taken it upon myself to make sure that Patrick Ryan never got the chance to abuse Laraine again and I was always there, always available so that he could do what he wanted to me and leave my little sister alone.

Neither of us talked about it but I got more and

more aggressive to poor Laraine. I remember one night she woke me up with her snivelling.

'Deb,' she whispered. 'Wake up, I've wet the bed.'

It still happened every now and then, and she was so ashamed that she was nearly nine and still messing herself.

'What do you want me to do about it?' I snapped. 'I'm not the one weeing myself like a baby every night.'

'Why are you being so mean to me, Deb?' she cried. 'Can I get in with you?'

'No, you can't,' I said. 'I don't want you peeing on my sheets too. Just leave me alone and go back to sleep.'

I knew I was being horrible and unkind but I just couldn't stop myself.

As I got older, I also struggled with the idea of puberty. I was horrified when my body started to change. I hated the idea of having breasts and I refused to wear a bra. So far Patrick Ryan had never been interested in anything up top because there was nothing to see, but I was worried it would give him something else to torment me with.

Starting my periods was a different matter, though. Some friends had got theirs already and I couldn't wait for it to happen. The risk of getting pregnant hadn't even entered my head: I just thought that if I was bleeding then perhaps Patrick Ryan wouldn't want to have sex with me and it might put him off.

By the time I was eleven, I was obsessed.

'When am I going to get mine, Mum?' I constantly asked. 'Do you think they'll come soon?'

'Don't worry about it, love. You'll have them for the rest of your life, believe me there's no rush.'

In the January, two months before I turned twelve, I was terrified when I woke up to find blood on my pyjamas one morning.

'Mum, I think I'm dying,' I said. 'I'm bleeding to death.'

'It's your period, silly,' she said.

I felt so grown up as I proudly helped myself to Mum's stash of sanitary towels.

That night after school, Alison was waiting on the stairs when we got home.

'Laraine, come and see,' she said. 'I've got a new doll's house.'

Laraine was up there like a shot as it had been a few months since we'd been to the flat; Mum was out working and, of course, I followed her up. As they played in the front room, Patrick Ryan soon turned his attentions to me.

He took me onto the landing and pulled my school trousers and pants down.

I saw his face change as he noticed the bloodstained sanitary towel stuck in my knickers.

'For fuck's sake,' he hissed. 'How long have you been having monthlies?'

'It's the first time,' I said, completely mortified that he'd seen it but at the same time glad.

But all my hopes that it would put him off were wrong. Nothing seemed to put that sick monster off. He still raped me that day although he didn't ejaculate inside me. Instead, he forced me to my knees and thrust his penis into my mouth. I closed my eyes and tried to focus on the fact that it would soon be over.

'Open your fucking eyes,' he spat.

But I didn't want to see what was happening. I didn't want to see that smug look of pleasure on his face as I knelt down in front of him.

'I said open your fucking eyes,' he growled, trying to prise my eyelids open with his dirty fingernails.

'I don't want to,' I mumbled.

But in the end I always did as he said. He yanked my chin up, so I was forced to look straight into his ugly face and that horrible wonky eye that turned inwards. Every single disgusting part of him was etched on my mind forever. Then, finally, it was over and he pulled his trousers up and calmly walked back into the front room. I didn't know it then but that was the last time that he would ever abuse me.

A couple of days later Mum sat us all down.

'I've got something important to tell you,' she said. 'Your father's due out of prison and the council think it's best that they move us to a new place so he can't find us.'

She explained that they'd found us a four-bedroom house, fifteen minutes away in Greenwich. I just sat there, completely stunned. I couldn't quite believe what I was hearing. I didn't care about how many bedrooms it had or where it was: all I cared about was the fact that we were moving. If we weren't going to live in this flat any more, that could only mean one thing. After suffering three years of hell at the hands of Patrick Ryan at last we were going to be free. Free of that monster, forever.

'When are we going?' I asked.

Mum must have seen the stunned look on my face.

'I know it's a bit of a shock, Debbie, but you'll get used to the idea,' she said. 'It's the best thing with your dad being released.

'Davina and Laraine can share, so you can have your own bedroom for once.'

'No,' I said. 'I think it's brilliant. I can't wait. When are we going?'

'By the end of the week,' said Mum.

It felt like Christmas, better than Christmas in fact. Five minutes, fifteen minutes, it didn't matter how short the distance was; the important thing was my father and Patrick Ryan wouldn't be able to get to me any more.

'It's great news, isn't it, Lal?' I said.

Laraine nodded and smiled. We didn't talk about it but we both knew what it meant.

Mum wasn't friendly with Wendy and she hated Patrick Ryan, so I was sure Laraine wouldn't keep in touch with Alison. Besides, she'd moved to my secondary school now and had friends of her own, so I knew that him and his family would be out of our lives for good. I was just so relieved.

Everything happened so quickly, it was a bit of a blur.

Two days later as we left for school, a man with a van was helping Mum load up our tatty old furniture into the back. Boxes of our things were piled up in the porch, just like that day in August all those years ago when Patrick Ryan had first moved in. I shuddered at the thought of that summer. Life had never been the same since then but now it was over at last.

The door to the upstairs flat was firmly closed as I went out of the front door for the last time. As I walked down the path, I stopped and turned around to have one final look at the place. I glanced at the upstairs flat but there was no one at the windows and the curtains were still closed.

'Good riddance, you bastard,' I muttered under my breath. 'I hate you.'

'Come on,' shouted Laraine. 'We're gonna be late.'

'Coming, Lal,' I sighed, closing the gate behind me, and as we ran down the road to school all I felt was utter relief.

But old habits die hard and even though we'd moved, I was still constantly looking over my shoulder, waiting for the next man to come along and abuse me. It had become part of my life and in some ways I had almost got used to it. Whenever we met a new neighbour or even a friend's dad I would think, 'Are you the one who's going to do it to me now?' I couldn't quite believe that it was over.

We made friends in our new street and although I was happy for them to come to our house, I would never go to theirs. I just couldn't risk it. Moving didn't help take away the anger I felt inside, either. I was still always looking out for Laraine too, especially as we were at the same school now.

One of my mates came rushing over to me at playtime one lunchtime.

'Some girl's hit your Laraine,' he told me.

'Where is she?' I asked.

'She's waiting outside the head teacher's office,' he said.

I ran straight there, rage building up inside me. Laraine was in the corridor in tears.

'Who hit you?' I asked and she pointed to a girl sat in a nearby classroom on her own. I marched straight over to her and punched her in the chest.

'Don't you ever hit my sister,' I shouted.

She hit me back, so I absolutely laid into her. I could hear Laraine screaming outside and eventually Mr Matthews ran in to pull us apart.

'Into my office now,' he yelled at me.

I knew I was in big trouble for beating up a girl two years younger than me. He phoned Mum and she came straight up to school.

'Debbie, what on earth have you been doing?' she said as she went into Mr Matthews' office.

'I don't know what's come over her,' I heard her say. 'We've been through a lot at home with her father over the years and her grandfather has recently passed away, which she took very badly.'

'She's always been very protective of her little sister.'

If only she knew the things that I'd done to protect Laraine, I thought. If only Laraine did too.

I could tell Mum was worried about me and I knew she was concerned about all of us. Davina was OK but David was still stammering and he and Laraine were withdrawn and struggling at school; I was angry and aggressive. Mum spoke to her GP and we were referred to family counselling at a health centre in Greenwich.

'We have to go once a week for ten weeks,' Mum told us.

I was dreading it. What if they asked me if I'd been abused? What if they could tell?

At the first session we met our counsellor, who was an American lady with frizzy hair called Lizzie. She seemed nice enough.

'You'll have a few sessions together as a family and then I'll see you all separately so that you have a chance to talk to me individually,' she said.

'You can tell me absolutely anything. Whatever you want to talk about.'

I knew the one thing I could never ever tell her was the truth. I was still terrified that no one would believe me and if they did then we might be taken into care again, or worse – Patrick Ryan would find us and carry out his threats. I was an expert at lying by then.

'Are you having any problems at school, Debbie?' she asked, during our one-to-one session.

'I've got into trouble a few times when I've lost it,' I shrugged.

'Why do you think you're feeling so angry?'

I told her exactly what I thought her and Mum wanted to hear.

'I've been very sad and angry since my Granddad George died so suddenly,' I said. 'And I was upset at the way Dad treated Mum. It was horrible to see him hurting her like that.'

'Good girl, Debbie,' she smiled. 'You're making good progress.'

If only she knew, what I wasn't telling her, the real reason why I was the way I was. But she didn't ask, so I didn't tell.

I wasn't worried about Laraine saying anything as she had never ever spoken about the abuse even to me, and she and David refused point-blank to say a word to the counsellor.

I was always on edge in those sessions, so it was a relief when our family counselling with Lizzie came to an end.

'I hope things get better,' I heard her say to Mum. 'It's clear that over the last few years you've all had a very unsettled home life, so I'm sure things will improve.'

I hoped she was right too.

Months passed and I tried my hardest to forget about our old flat in Blackheath and everything that had gone on there. Thankfully Michael and Shane didn't go to the same school as us, but I still lived in fear of seeing Patrick Ryan again. Andrew, one of my good mates, still lived in our old street but I had stopped going to his house when we moved. It was hard, as he was always inviting me round. It was torture too, because he had loads of pets and he knew how much I loved animals.

'Come round after school one night and see my mice,' he said. 'Go on, Debbie. I've got a new duck too.'

'A duck?' I laughed. 'Oh, all right then.'

It made me uneasy going back to that street and being near our old flat again but Andrew's place was further down the road and what were the chances of me seeing Patrick Ryan again?

I was still terrified as I wandered along that familiar street towards Andrew's house.

You're OK, Debbie, he's not here, I told myself. He can't hurt you any more.

But as I walked down the road, I saw a figure coming towards me. Fear ran through me and I stopped, suddenly rooted to the spot.

It couldn't be him, could it?

But I would have recognised him anywhere. The same scruffy leather jacket and tatty jeans, round sunglasses, hands in his pockets, slightly stooped. I panicked, didn't know what to do.

I didn't want to cross the road as I thought it would only draw attention to myself and he might run after me. So, with my heart racing, I put my head down and kept on walking towards Patrick Ryan. I could hear his footsteps coming closer and closer.

Don't look up at him. Just carry on walking.

I held my breath and seconds later we passed each other in the street. As if we were two strangers who had never met, he didn't say a word or even acknowledge me. He just walked straight past. I didn't even see his face or know if he'd shown any reaction because I was too busy focusing on the pavement.

I felt sick and totally shaken up. I needed to get away, as far away as possible from that street and Patrick Ryan. So I kept on walking, right past Andrew's house and went the long way home. I kept looking behind me all the way just to check he wasn't following me. Thankfully, there was no sign of him.

I vowed never to go back to that street again and I never did. Well, not for another thirty-five years.

Chapter 9

Opposites

I could see the huddle of girls in the corner of the playground and before I even got near them, I knew exactly what they would be talking about.

'This weekend I'm definitely gonna do it with Darren,' I overheard one blonde girl say proudly, and they all screamed with excitement.

'I can't believe I'm still a virgin,' another one chipped in. 'I'd like to do it in the summer, on a beach, I think.'

'Oh, Chelle, that's so romantic,' sighed her friend. 'Did you hear that Becky gave Brian Smith a blow job at the school disco last week?'

I felt sick listening to them and their 'sex talk'. I was seventeen now and all the girls my age in the lower sixth seemed to be interested in was who was getting off with whom, who had touched them up or who they were going to sleep with.

One of the girls caught me staring and shouted over, 'Oi, Debbie, you're not a virgin, are you? I bet you popped your cherry ages ago, didn't yer?'

'No, I bloody well didn't,' I snapped angrily and they all laughed.

'She's a weirdo,' I heard one of them say as I walked off.

'A dyke more like,' another replied and they all sniggered.

But I didn't care what they said about me. I had no interest in standing around with them gossiping about lipstick, clothes and boys. After being abused, I didn't trust men and the thought of having sex or even just kissing one didn't just make my stomach turn, it frightened the living daylights out of me. I wasn't interested in the same things most teenage girls at my school were. I liked swimming or going out on my bike to the local BMX ramps with my friends, who were mostly boys. I felt like an outsider with the girls, but the boys just treated me like one of the lads, which I liked as I still hated everything about being a woman.

I normally avoided going out at night, but one Friday Laraine persuaded me to come to a party at the local youth club.

'I'm not interested, Lal. I'm supposed to be going swimming,' I told her.

'Don't be such a spoilsport. Come to the party, you might enjoy it,' she said.

Laraine was almost sixteen now and we couldn't have been more different if we'd tried. The shy, scared, withdrawn little girl had long gone and she had grown into a bubbly, outgoing teenager. She was everything I wasn't – pretty, popular, feminine. She liked getting dressed up and going down to the youth club, flirting with boys and getting tipsy on Strongbow. Laraine was always the life and soul of the party whereas people would take one look at my sulky face and said, 'You should be more like your sister.'

It really rattled me even though I tried not to let it get me down. I knew it was mean of me to be angry with her as she'd been through some awful things too.

'OK,' I sighed. 'I'll come.'

'Great,' smiled Laraine. 'We'll have an ace time, Deb, I promise.'

Laraine put on some blue mascara in the mirror while I pulled on a pair of boy's jeans and one of David's baggy sweatshirts that I'd nicked from his bedroom.

'Oh, Deb,' she sighed. 'Don't go out in that baggy shapeless stuff you always wear. People will think you're a bloke!

'You'll never get a boyfriend looking like that.'

'Good,' I said.

Little did my sister know, but that was the biggest compliment that she could ever pay me. That's exactly why I dressed the way I did.

'You know everyone at school thinks you're a lesbian, Deb?' she told me.

'Don't bother me one bit,' I said, shrugging my shoulders. 'They can think what they like. Anyway, it's better than being a slag like some people.'

As soon as the words were out of my mouth, I regretted them.

'Sometimes, Deb, you can be a real bitch,' said Laraine with tears in her eyes.

I didn't mean to be horrible but sometimes I still really resented her. Laraine didn't know what had happened to me with our father and Patrick Ryan, and she had been through hell, too, but she had coped with being abused so differently to me. Ever since she'd been old enough, she'd had boyfriends and I guessed that she was probably sexually active, like most of the girls at school.

Laraine seemed to need the reassurance of having a boyfriend and I knew underneath it all, she just wanted to be loved. But it was completely different to the way I felt. I couldn't imagine ever being in a relationship or wanting to sleep with a man. The only bloke I trusted was David, my brother. So I really didn't care if the whole school thought that I was a lesbian.

Let them think what they like, I told myself. At least then lads would leave me alone and want nothing to do with me.

The party at the youth club was as bad as I'd expected. There were couples snogging in every corner or draped over each other on the dance floor, wandering hands everywhere. Boys never tried to chat me up because of the way I looked but one spotty lad came sauntering over to me.

He's brave, I thought. Or else he'd been put up to it by his mates as a joke.

'Do you fancy a dance?' he said. 'I love a bit of Spandau Ballet, me.'

'Just fuck off, will you,' I said bluntly.

An angry look flashed across his face.

'Don't speak to me like that, you dyke.'

'Well, then you know why I'm not interested,' I snapped, and he soon wandered off.

I came across as so tough and hard-faced but really it was all an act. It was a big cover-up to try and disguise the fact that inside I still felt like a frightened little girl, terrified that someone was going to hurt me again.

'Oh, Debbie, you're angry all the time and so hard to get along with,' Mum would tell me. 'Why can't you be more like your sister?'

I knew I was being argumentative but I couldn't stop myself. I was determined that no one was going to pick on me ever again. If there was a fight, it was because I had started it: I was the one in control.

I knew Mum worried about me. We were tucking into a dinner of beef stew one night when she glanced over at me and smiled.

'What?' I said.

'I was just thinking you look so much better with a bit of weight back on. Don't she, girls?'

Laraine and Davina nodded in agreement.

'Yeah, Deb, you got a cracking little figure,' said Laraine. 'You should show it off more.'

It was the worst thing anyone could have said to me and it was like waving a red flag in front of a bull. I'd been a chubby kid but in my early teens I'd gone off food. It sounds strange but because of the disgusting things Patrick Ryan had made me do to him, I hated the feeling of anything being in my mouth. For years I'd just picked at meals and I'd got really skinny. But with all the sport I'd been doing recently, I was genuinely hungry, so I'd started eating properly again and had put on a bit of weight without noticing.

'Hey, Debbie, with a few curves you might even find yourself a husband before long,' said David.

He was only being nice but I hated compliments. I didn't want to look 'nice' as that might mean that I looked attractive to men.

'I need the loo,' I mumbled, going off to the bathroom.

I stared at myself in the mirror. I looked at my short hair and the baggy boy's clothes I was wearing. What had Patrick Ryan made me become? But I didn't want to look nice, I couldn't risk the thought of a man trying it on with me. So I closed my eyes and stuck two fingers down the back of my throat. I gagged and retched and eventually I was sick.

After that, I'd make myself sick after every meal. It felt good to be in control and I liked the fact that I was losing weight again. No one ever suspected anything and as far as my family was aware, I was eating all my meals. Mum would look so pleased as she cleared my clean plate away, not realising what I was up to in the bathroom while she did the washing up.

I hated everything about myself. If anyone ever

tried to compliment me or said I looked nice or smart, I wouldn't wear those clothes again. As I got older and approached my eighteenth birthday, it became even more apparent to me how wrong the foster parents, my father and then Patrick Ryan had been to do those awful things to me. I was just a child for God's sake and I knew now what a huge betrayal of trust and power it had been. I just couldn't forget the past, no matter how hard I tried.

I might have put on this hard-faced act but I was only human and soon the strain of pretending to be like that all the time did start to get to me. I'd stayed on in the sixth form to do English A-level and wherever I went in school people would whisper about me or call me 'Debbie the dyke'. At first it had seemed like the easiest option to let everyone think I was a lesbian, but I was getting fed up of being the butt of everyone's jokes. So I came up with a plan.

My brother David had a friend who he was always mentioning to me.

For months he'd been telling me, 'Ryan really fancies you. Will you go out with him? Go on, Deb, give him a chance, he's a nice bloke.'

I'd always told him where to go, of course, but suddenly I changed my mind. I thought if I went out with a lad, even for a few weeks, it might shut people up for a bit and they would leave me alone.

So the next time David told me that Ryan had been asking about me again, I said, 'Oh, that's nice of him. Do you think he'd like to go for a walk in Greenwich Park with me sometime?'

I could see David was surprised that I'd changed my mind.

'Oh er, all right then, Debbie, if you're sure then I'll get him to ring you.'

Ryan seemed like a decent enough bloke although I didn't find him in the least bit attractive. He was tall and skinny and he had long ginger hair. We used to go out for a walk or he'd come round to our house and watch telly, and even though I didn't fancy him, we got along OK. Sometimes he would try and kiss me but I would just gently push him away.

My plan worked. The lesbian rumours stopped and I could see how relieved everyone was that I was going out with a bloke and was finally 'normal' in their eyes.

We'd been going out with each other a few months and were up in my bedroom one day, playing tapes. We were sat together on the bed when Ryan leaned over and said, 'You know I really like you, Debbie?'

I just froze. I knew instantly that he was going to try it on with me.

He pushed me back onto the bed and before I could stop him, put his tongue into my mouth. I could feel him stroking my leg through my tracksuit bottoms, his hand getting higher and higher up my thigh. My heart started pounding with fear as I felt his fingers between my legs. Just like the foster parents had done, just like my father, just like evil Patrick Ryan. Suddenly I was that frightened little girl again.

My instincts kicked in and I knew I had to get him off me before he went any further. I managed to push him away and I reached across and opened the top drawer of my bedside table. I fumbled around until I felt the cold chill of metal against my fingers.

'What the—?' gasped Ryan as I flicked the Stanley knife out of its cover and pressed the blade to his cheek.

'If you ever dare touch me again then I will stab you with this,' I said. 'And believe me, I mean every word.'

I think it was my calmness that freaked him out even more.

'You mad bitch,' he said, running to the door.

As soon as he'd gone, the calm, controlled Debbie disappeared and I started shaking like a leaf. I could hear Ryan shouting at Laraine downstairs.

'Your sister's mental,' he said. 'She pulled a fucking knife on me. She's supposed to be my girlfriend.'

I didn't feel safe until I heard the front door slam behind him.

Laraine came in to see me.

'He didn't look very happy,' she said. 'Are you OK?'

'Yep,' I nodded. 'I don't think you'll be seeing much of Ryan any more.'

'Oh, Deb,' she sighed. 'I wish you could meet someone special.'

Ryan was obviously not very happy that I'd shunned

his advances and over the next few days he managed to spread rumours all round the school that I definitely was a lesbian. I don't think there was anyone in Greenwich who didn't know that I was a 'frigid little dyke' as he'd so nicely put it. I tried not to let it get to me but it was hard.

'Is it true what he's saying, Debbie?' David asked me. 'I don't mind. If you prefer women then that's none of my business.'

'Don't be stupid,' I told him. 'He's just pissed off that I didn't put out for him.'

'Well, it's going all round school,' said Laraine. 'It's really embarrassing, Deb.'

Even my own family was ashamed of me.

'You can all believe what you want to believe,' I shouted before storming out.

That night I took myself off to bed early, but before long something woke me from my sleep. I could feel a heavy weight pressing down on me, so heavy that I couldn't breathe. Hands were holding my wrists down so I couldn't move.

Oh God, someone was on top of me.

I tried to struggle but I was powerless. Then I felt hot breath on my neck and smelled that familiar pungent smell: stale beer mixed with sweat.

And suddenly he was there in my bedroom. Patrick Ryan.

'Open your fucking eyes, you little whore.'

'No!' I screamed. 'No! Get off me. You can't hurt me any more.'

But he could and as he forced himself inside me, I felt that horrible, burning pain that felt like I was being ripped in two...

The next thing I knew Laraine was stood by my bed in her pyjamas, shaking me awake.

'Deb,' she whispered. 'Deb, are you OK? I heard you shouting. You must have been having a nightmare.'

'What?' I mumbled as I started to come round. 'Where is he? Has he gone?'

'Who?' she said. 'Deb, there's no one here.'

My head was spinning but slowly I started to breathe normally again as I told myself over and over again that it wasn't real and Patrick Ryan couldn't hurt me any more.

'Are you sure you're OK?' Laraine asked, and I nodded.

But the truth was, I was far from it. I would never ever forget what Patrick Ryan had done to me but for years I'd tried to push him to the back of my mind. His voice, his smell, his dirty clothes, the disgusting things that he'd done to me. But Ryan trying it on with me had triggered something in my mind and brought it all back as if it had happened yesterday. I was that bewildered, frightened little girl again.

Most nights after that were the same. I'd feel like Patrick Ryan was on top of me, squeezing the air out of my lungs as he thrust into me again and again. It was all so frighteningly real. I'd wake up sweating and shaking, petrified and unable to breathe. Then I'd stagger to the bathroom, where I would be violently sick.

After weeks and weeks of flashbacks and nightmares it all got too much. I was still throwing up most of my meals and I was down to six stone. One morning I woke up and I literally couldn't get out of bed. I sat there and sobbed for hours.

'What is it, Debbie?' said Mum. 'What's the matter?'

'I can't get out of bed,' I cried. 'I can't do it any more.'

'I'm going to call the doctor,' she said, looking worried.

The GP diagnosed me with depression and put me on some medication. It took weeks and weeks but very slowly, it started to help.

I could see Laraine was really worried about me.

'What is it, Deb?' she said. 'Why are you so unhappy?'

For a second I thought about telling her what our dad had done and what Patrick Ryan had put me through too to protect her. But I couldn't, the words just got stuck in my throat.

'I don't know, Lal,' I sobbed.

I'd never told Laraine because I didn't want her to know. I still felt so ashamed, so dirty and disgusted about what he had done to me. I didn't want her to blame herself either.

Although Laraine and I were so different, after everything we had been through together we did have an unspoken bond. I would still look out for her and I always knew where she was and with whom. My worst fear was that she would be treated badly by a bloke, so I was worried when she turned sixteen and got her first serious boyfriend. Danny was twenty-one and one of Dave's friends from the garage where they worked as mechanics.

The age difference bothered me. At seventeen I still saw Laraine as a child and I didn't want her to be taken advantage of.

'Isn't he a bit old for you, Lal?' I said.

'He's lovely,' she sighed and I could see that she absolutely adored him.

But as the months passed and we all got to know Danny and saw how nicely he treated Laraine, I warmed to him a bit more. I knew that the one thing Laraine wanted in the world was to get married.

'I can't wait to settle down and have kids,' she always told me.

I was really happy for her but I wasn't envious. I didn't need anyone in my life, I didn't want to rely on anybody.

Danny used to see Laraine on certain nights each week but after they'd been going out for a while, he started making excuses.

'I don't understand it, Deb,' she confided in me. 'Do you think he's going off me?'

She was really upset. I was no expert on blokes but in my mind I was worried that he was seeing someone else. Then I noticed something else. The nights Danny was ringing up and saying that he couldn't make it coincided with the nights that Laraine would mention her best friend Sonia was going out. She and Laraine had been best mates for years and she was always round our house. The pair of them enjoyed getting dressed up and going out.

That can't be right, I told myself. She wouldn't do that to her best friend, would she? I'd just put two and two together and got five.

But I couldn't get rid of my suspicions. One night Laraine mentioned that Danny had cancelled another date with her.

'I'm so fed up, Deb,' she said. 'I can't even invite Sonia round because she's out tonight too.'

Sonia only lived around the corner from us so just to make sure, I decided I was going to follow her. She called round to our house before she went out.

'I'm just off up the youth club but I've got nothing to wear,' she said. 'Can I borrow some of your clothes, Laraine?'

'Course you can,' she said. 'Come in.'

She lent Sonia one of her dresses and even did her make-up for her. Surely I'd got it wrong? But as I watched Sonia saunter up the street in her high heels and Laraine's clothes, I saw a car waiting for her around the corner: Danny's car. I couldn't believe it when I saw her jump into the passenger seat and lean over for a passionate kiss.

All I could think was poor Laraine. Both of them were taking advantage of her kind, sweet nature. Danny was her first love and Sonia was her best mate. I knew she was going to be devastated.

The next day Sonia came round after school.

'Did you have a nice time last night?' asked Laraine.

'Oh yeah, I just went up to the youth club,' she said. 'Nothing special.'

But I couldn't just sit there and let Sonia lie to Laraine like that.

'OK, Sonia,' I said. 'I think you need to tell my sister where you really were last night. Or should I say *who* you were with?'

Her face fell and she looked guilty as hell.

'What do you mean, Debbie?' she said. 'I told you I was at the youth club.'

'I said tell her where you've really been.'

Laraine looked confused.

'What's this all about, Deb? Why are you being so mean to Sonia?'

But Sonia wouldn't tell Laraine so in the end, I did. I knew she was going to be devastated but I just couldn't sit there and watch her being deceived like that.

'I can't believe it,' she sobbed. 'I thought he loved me.'

'I'm so sorry,' said Sonia. 'It just happened.'

Laraine was gutted and unsurprisingly she and Sonia fell out really badly over it.

It took Laraine a long time to get over that and it really knocked her confidence. But finally, months later, she met someone else. Brendan Delgiudice also worked with David. She'd been talking to him on and off when he'd come home from work with David and they started seeing each other. She'd finally come to accept that Sonia and Danny were together and in a serious relationship and it was nice to see her happy again.

'Wouldn't you like a boyfriend, Deb?' Laraine asked me one night. 'Don't you want to get married and have children?'

'I'll have the kids but I don't want the bloke that goes with it,' I told her.

And that's what I always said. Laraine didn't understand as she didn't know what Patrick Ryan had done to me. There were many times over the years that a tiny part of me was tempted to tell her. But I didn't. Even then, all those years later, I was still ashamed. I felt dirty and disgusting and I blamed myself. I didn't deserve to be happy. No, whatever happened, I knew I could never ever tell anyone what I'd been through.

Chapter 10
New Beginnings

I took one look at the tiny bundle lying in the see-through cot and my heart melted. From his wrinkled little face to his legs which were scrunched up close to his body like a frog's, he was the most perfect thing that I'd ever seen.

'Oh, Lal,' I sighed, stroking his cheek. 'He's beautiful.'

'He's a little smasher, isn't he?' Laraine beamed.

I'd come to see her in Greenwich hospital just after she'd had her first child, a son they'd called Jordan. It'd been a long labour and Laraine must have been shattered but she looked the happiest I'd ever seen.

She was twenty-two now and she and Brendan had been together for four years. I knew being a mum would be the making of my little sister as she'd always wanted children.

'Can I give my new nephew a cuddle, then?' I asked her.

'Course,' she said.

Carefully I lifted Jordan from the cot and he nestled in the crook of my arm. I buried my nose in his white terry towelling Babygro and breathed in that sweet newborn smell.

'You're a natural, Deb,' said Laraine. 'You should have one of your own.'

'I wish,' I sighed.

I longed to be a mum with all my heart but I couldn't bear the thought of having to sleep with a man. I was pleased Laraine was so happy and settled but sometimes I still felt a tiny bit resentful that she had moved on despite everything that had happened with Patrick Ryan. But I knew that people dealt with things in different ways and she'd been through so much too.

I felt like I couldn't get over the past as the abuse was always at the back of my mind. If there were any films or programmes on telly with sex in them then I couldn't watch them.

I came across as a real man-hater too. I constantly told David, 'The only man I'll ever love is you.'

'Oh, Debbie, you'll change your tune one day,' he said.

But I was convinced I wouldn't.

Davina and David had both got married too by now, so it was just me left living at home with Mum. I did whatever I could to earn money – child-minding, working in a shop, cleaning. One of my cleaning jobs was for a woman called Liz who ran a bed and breakfast. She was single like me, although unlike me, she was desperate to find a fella.

'Don't you want a boyfriend, Debbie?' she said.

'No, I'm not interested,' I told her time and time again.

But for some stupid reason I let her talk me into going to a singles' night at a wine bar in Sidcup.

'It's a laugh, I've been there loads of times,' she said.

'Alright, alright, I'll come,' I sighed, just to get her off my back.

As soon as I set foot in the place, I regretted it as it was full of lecherous old men. One fat, bald guy was sat there leering at all the women having a dance. I clocked him straight away but I still couldn't believe it when I walked past and felt him pinch my bum. Quick as a flash, I turned round and punched him in the face.

He was so shocked, he didn't say a word.

'What right is it of yours to touch me when I wasn't asking for it?' I yelled.

'Debbie, what the hell are you doing?' said Liz, dragging me away from him. 'All he did was touch your arse. It's a singles' night, for God's sake.'

'That doesn't mean it's OK,' I said.

A few seconds later two burly bouncers marched towards me.

'Uh-oh, I think I'm going to get slung out,' I said.

They grabbed my arms and escorted me off the premises.

'Have you had a few too many, darling?' one of them asked me.

'No,' I said. 'I'm not even drinking. I've only had a Coke.'

They could tell I wasn't drunk, so they decided to let me go.

'It's your lucky night,' one of them said. 'If you apologise to that gentleman then we'll let you back in.'

But I was unrepentant.

'If you let me back in then I'll finish what I started,' I said.

I wasn't going to let some fat, bald old bloke touch me up just because he felt like it. I was determined that no man would ever take advantage of me again.

That was the first and last time I stepped into one of those places. Liz stayed at the wine bar and a few days later she sacked me.

'You're such an angry, aggressive person, Debbie,' she told me, and to be honest, she was probably right.

The lesbian rumours had been going round about me for years so I decided what the heck, I would pretend to be what everybody thought I was. Although I knew in my heart that I wasn't really attracted to women, I started going to gay bars. I realised that they were the only places where I could have a night out, feel safe and not be bothered by sleazy men trying to take advantage of me. Sometimes I'd get chatted up by a woman and we'd talk for hours but at the end of the night, I'd always make my excuses and leave.

I also decided that it was time to get a proper job. I saw a position advertised to work in the warehouse of a posh department store in London, so I decided to go for it. I was really chuffed when I got an interview.

'You can have the job but are you sure you want to

work in the warehouse, dear?' said the man interviewing me. 'We've got another vacancy on the shop floor that you might be more interested in.'

He explained that it was on one of the expensive make-up counters.

'There are sales-related bonuses and the uniform is a very smart navy blue dress.'

I just laughed.

'I ain't doing that,' I said. 'I want a proper man's job.'

I think he was a bit taken aback, but I enjoyed doing manual work. I wanted to be in the warehouse lifting heavy loads and driving around in a forklift truck. I even liked the uniform, which was a polo shirt and trousers. I was one of three women who worked there and the rest of the lads were a good bunch. I'd been there a few months when the manager came over to see me.

'We've got a new starter coming in today, so I want you to show him the ropes,' he told me.

The new bloke was called Rob Grafham. He was stood in reception in a shirt and tie, which made me smile.

'You're going to get a bit mucky in the warehouse wearing that,' I joked.

'I thought I'd better look smart for my first day,' he said.

We chatted for a while and he told me he was from Charlton. When he described where he lived, I recognised it straight away.

'I know that street,' I said. 'It's up the road from where my granddad used to be.'

He was a year older than me and it turned out that we'd both gone to Blackheath Bluecoats high school although neither of us recognised the other.

I had to train Rob in the warehouse and work with him until he'd picked the job up. Straight away we got on and soon became friends. We had a laugh and I liked him and felt comfortable with him because he never made any remarks about the way I looked or dressed. I never heard him making any sexual innuendos like a lot of lads did, either. He was kind too and would sometimes offer to help me out on jobs.

'I'll lift that for you,' he said one day when he saw me struggling with some heavy pallets.

'No, I can do it, thanks,' I told him.

Being the stubborn fool that I am I was desperate to prove I could do it despite the fact I nearly broke my back a couple of times!

We got the same train into London of a morning and we started going to the pub after work with some of the other blokes from the warehouse. We even shared the same hobbies, like cycling and swimming.

'Do you fancy going for a bike ride at the weekend, Deb?' he asked one afternoon.

I smiled at hearing him call me Deb. It was only Laraine who called me that but I liked it.

'All right then,' I said. 'Although be warned, I'll probably beat you.'

After we'd known each other for eight months Rob invited me to come to his parents' silver wedding anniversary party.

'I'd really like you to meet my mum and dad,' he said.

I was flattered that he had asked me as all his family were there. His mum Shirley and dad Eddie were really nice.

'You know Rob really likes you,' Shirley told me as we stood chatting.

I felt my cheeks go red.

'Yes, he's a good friend to me too,' I said.

I'd made a real effort to look smart for the party. I'd bought a new white blouse to wear rather than my usual man's shirt and a black jacket and trousers. Halfway through the night one of Rob's great uncles came over to chat to us. I could tell he was drunk.

'Uncle Ray, I'd like you to meet Debbie,' said Rob.

He looked me up and down, frowned and said, 'You look like a dyke.'

I was used to it by then, so I just tried to laugh it off but I could see Rob was fuming.

'You've got a bloody cheek saying that to her,' he told him.

'I'm really sorry about that,' he said when he'd gone.

'It's OK, people have called me a lot worse,' I smiled.

That was Rob all over. He accepted me for what I was and he wasn't ashamed to be seen with me. He never asked me if I was a lesbian or quizzed me about boyfriends. I felt so at ease with him and I grew to really trust him.

He started to open up to me too.

'I'm not looking for a relationship,' I told him. 'I'm just not interested.'

'Me neither, it always ends in tears,' he said.

Rob explained how he had been engaged to someone but she had called it off a few weeks before the wedding and he'd been devastated.

That New Year's Eve we were having a party at home, so I invited Rob. All the family were there and he met David, Davina, Mum and Laraine.

'I like your boyfriend,' teased Laraine, giving me a wink.

'Give over, Lal,' I said. 'We're just mates.'

I don't know what made me say it but at the end of the night I turned round to Rob and asked him, 'Do you want to stay over?'

I was miserable, I knew he was miserable. It was New Year and I didn't want to be on my own.

'No, don't worry,' he said. 'I think I'll just go home.'

I was upset as it had taken a lot of guts for me to ask him that. I didn't want anything to happen, I just didn't want him to leave. That was the first time I think I realised that I wanted us to be more than just friends. I liked the idea of having a boyfriend but it also terrified me.

There was one other thing that made me see I'd fallen for Rob. He had a friend called Karen, who he always talked about. There was nothing going on between them but whenever we weren't together, he seemed to be with her. I could feel my heckles rising whenever he mentioned her, and I realised that I was jealous. It was pathetic, really. I'd never even met the girl, and I knew they were just friends, but I hated her. Rob was the first man, besides David, that I trusted and felt safe with and I knew then I didn't want to lose him. Thankfully he must have felt the same because over the next few months, we became boyfriend and girlfriend. There was no big conversation or announcement to people: we just sort of fell into it. Everyone had already assumed that we were a couple anyway.

Just before Christmas, Rob and I were at work when we had to take some clothes up to the shop floor that we'd priced up and put security tags on. We both had great big pallets of stuff so we decided to go together and pile them all up on one truck.

As we were heading to womenswear, we walked through the bridal department, where there was a wedding dress on display on a mannequin. Rob stopped next to it.

'That's nice, Deb,' he said, pointing it out to me.

'I wouldn't be seen dead in one of them dresses,' I said.

'Why not?' he asked. 'I think you'd look lovely. Why don't you try one on later?'

'No way,' I said. 'They're gross.'

'Well, I think it would suit you,' he said.

I didn't think any more of it until a few days later on Christmas Eve when Rob took me out for a meal to a Greek restaurant in Greenwich. We were sitting there when suddenly he grabbed my hand.

'I love you, Debbie,' he told me.

'I know you do,' I said. 'I love you, too.'

'No, I haven't finished. There's something I want to ask you.'

Then he paused and said, 'Will you marry me?'

I was stunned but so pleased.

'Of course I will,' I smiled.

He'd saved up for months and bought me a beautiful diamond cluster engagement ring that he'd chosen from a shop on Oxford Street.

We went home and told my family: they were all pleased and I think very relieved. Rob got on well with all of them.

'I'm so happy for you, Deb,' said Laraine. 'I always knew that you'd meet someone one day.'

'Well, you might have but I didn't,' I joked.

But I also had something serious to ask her.

'When we get married, Lal, I'd really like it if you would be my chief bridesmaid.'

'Aw, that would be brilliant,' she said, throwing her arms around me.

But despite my happiness at getting engaged, at the back of my mind there was one big stumbling block. I loved Rob and I wanted to marry him more than anything but I was terrified of having sex with him. I knew it had to happen sooner or later but I was dreading it.

I know you're thinking why didn't I come clean and tell him what I'd been through? But I couldn't. I'd never told a single soul about the abuse that I'd suffered as a child. I was worried that if I told Rob then he'd think I was easy or see me as 'soiled goods'. What if he ran a mile and didn't want anything more to do with me? This was the one and only relationship in my life that mattered and I didn't want to mess it up.

After we got engaged we needed to start saving up for the wedding, so Rob moved in with me at Mum's. Occasionally we were intimate but we didn't have sex.

'Not until we're married,' I would tell him.

It was a convenient excuse but Rob respected that and he never questioned it, which made me love him even more.

We planned a big church wedding for the following September.

'What you gonna wear, Deb?' said Laraine. 'Don't tell me you're going to walk up the aisle in white trousers and a shirt?'

Her and Mum laughed but I knew they were secretly worried.

I probably would have worn a suit, given half the chance, but I knew how much it meant to Rob to see me in a wedding dress and I thought if I was going to do this properly then I wanted to wear one. But the idea still terrified me.

'The last time I wore a dress I was nine years old,' I told him.

I remembered exactly as it was around the time when Patrick Ryan had started abusing me. I could even see it in my head – a little paisley mini dress with a Peter Pan collar.

'Well, if you're that nervous I'll come with you if you want,' Rob told me.

'Will you?' I said. 'You'd really do that for me?'

So the next weekend Rob and I went to Berketex on Oxford Street. I could see all the shop assistants thought it was a bit odd that I was bringing my fiancé to help choose my dress.

'Isn't it bad luck if he sees it before the wedding?' one of them joked.

'Aw, Deb doesn't believe in all that claptrap,' Rob told her.

It did feel strange trying all these long white dresses on and looking in the mirror. I'd spent so many years trying to make myself look as unattractive as possible and now I was trying on these big, extravagant gowns so that I could be the centre of attention for a day.

'I don't want anything too big and puffy,' I told Rob.

In the end he helped me pick out a lovely fitted dress with lace sleeves and a long train.

'You look beautiful,' he said.

I didn't think I'd ever feel beautiful but I liked it.

Laraine came with me for a final fitting and to pick up her and Davina's peach satin bridesmaid dresses.

'Oh, Deb,' she said. 'You look gorgeous.'

'I don't feel like me in it,' I told her.

Maybe that wasn't such a bad thing. This was my new start, my chance to be happy for once.

But on the morning of the wedding, I was a wreck. Everyone else seemed so excited but I just felt sick. Laraine turned up at 6am, clutching a bottle of bubbly.

'Wake up, Deb, it's your big day,' she said, but I didn't want to get out of bed.

David was giving me away and later when everyone else had gone on ahead to St Luke's Church in Charlton Village where we were having the service, it was just the two of us left at home.

I was sick with nerves. Not about marrying Rob but the fact that I was going to feel like such a fraud walking down the aisle in that white dress. There was such a big part of my life that my husband-to-be didn't know about and I was worried that I wouldn't be able to be a proper wife to him. What if I couldn't ever bring myself to have sex?

I was annoyed that even on my wedding day the past was coming back to haunt me. There had been so many moments when I'd wanted to tell Rob, almost to test him to see what his reaction would be, but in the end I'd always chickened out. I couldn't run the risk of losing him.

David could see how worried and upset I looked and he came over and put his arm around me.

'You know you don't have to go through with it, Debbie, if you don't want,' he said. 'You don't have to prove anything to people. If you've got doubts then you don't have to do it.

'I'll go down to the church for you and tell everyone it's all off.'

I could see he was worried that I was doing something that I didn't want.

'I'm honestly not a lesbian, Dave,' I told him. 'I want to get married. I love Rob, I really do. I'm just nervous, that's all.'

We were an hour late by the time we arrived at the church and I could see Laraine's worried face as we pulled up outside.

'Where have you been?' she shouted. 'Get a move on, Deb! Poor Rob's sweating in there.'

I was shaking with nerves as I heard the organ start playing and I took David's arm.

'You can do it, Sis,' he said. 'You look beautiful.'

We walked up the aisle followed by Davina and then Laraine. Laraine had refused to put her glasses on but she was as blind as a bat without them. I'd almost got to the front of the church when I felt a dragging on my dress and heard a loud ripping noise. I turned around to see Laraine had stood on my train with her white stiletto. There was a big hole in it and it had started to come away from my dress.

'Oh, bloody hell, Lal, you've ripped my train,' I said.

'Debbie!' whispered Rob as I reached the front. 'You can't swear in church.'

I think even the vicar had heard, as he gave me a funny look!

Thankfully, I managed to get through my vows and it was a relief to finally be married. Afterwards we had a reception in the church hall and Rob and I had our first dance to 'Endless Love' by Diana Ross and Lionel Richie. As Rob wrapped his arms around me and we swayed to the music, I felt so safe.

'I love you,' I told him. 'You're my best friend.'

I meant it but I still felt so guilty that I was hiding so much from him, and the thought of having to consummate our marriage was preying on my mind all day.

That night we went back to a lovely hotel in Blackheath. We had the bridal suite and there was a bottle of champagne in an ice bucket waiting for us. But I couldn't relax as I knew tonight I was going to have to have sex.

It's now or never, I told myself. I had to get this over and done with and prove to myself that I could do it. I necked a glass of champagne for Dutch courage and then got into bed. Rob and I cuddled up.

'I love you so much, Deb,' he said, stroking my face.

I knew this was it and I was shaking like a leaf. This was the first time in my life that I had chosen to have sex with someone and I was dreading it. I was worried that it would bring back all the bad memories and I would have a panic attack. Or worse, what if I freaked out and attacked Rob?

Please don't let him do the same things that Patrick Ryan did to me, I said to myself as I closed my eyes. I was absolutely terrified.

I know it sounds crude but I couldn't bear the thought of Rob being on top of me. I was worried it would make me feel like I was trapped, like I couldn't get away. So I made sure I was on top. I didn't have a clue what I was doing but at least I felt like I was in control.

I let Rob take the lead. I just closed my eyes and willed it to be over as soon as possible. I was so scared that he would sense my fear or say something, but I must have hidden it well.

'Are you OK?' he whispered afterwards, and I nodded.

You see it was the truth: it really was OK. Rob had been so gentle and loving and it was so much better than I'd been expecting. I turned away so he wouldn't see the tears running down my face.

You've done it, Debbie, I told myself.

It felt like a real achievement. I'd refused to let Patrick Ryan ruin the one relationship that mattered to me. If it had then he would have won. I didn't know if I would ever be able to enjoy sex but with Rob, I felt safe and loved.

'Are you crying?' asked Rob.

'Yes,' I told him. 'But they're happy tears.'

For the first time in my life I had hope for the future. Perhaps now at last I could try and forget the past and finally be happy.

Chapter 11

A Mum at Last

The truth was, Rob had saved me. I wasn't angry with the world any more. Suddenly I was things that I never ever thought I would be – settled, content and, dare I say it, happy for the first time in my life.

I was also a woman obsessed. Obsessed with having a baby.

'I want to have kids as soon as possible,' I told Rob straight after the wedding.

'Deb, we need to save up first,' he said.

I'd always wanted to be a mum but I was in such a rush because I was convinced that I wouldn't be able to have children. After being raped at such a young age, I was worried that I was damaged internally. Getting pregnant was the only way to prove to myself that I was a normal woman.

But I knew Rob was right, so we both got an extra job at a cash and carry warehouse called Makro and worked every hour God sent. In the meantime, I went to see the family doctor about going on the pill.

The GP took my blood pressure and asked me a few questions. She rattled down the long list – my age, my weight, family medical history.

'From what age were you sexually active?' she asked.

'Nine,' I said straight away without thinking.

The doctor paused and looked up at me.

'Pardon?' she said. 'I think I misheard you there. How old were you when you first started having sex?'

I was completely mortified and couldn't believe I'd just blurted that out so casually.

'Oh, er, sorry, I mean nineteen,' I mumbled.

It was at times like that I realised what had become normal to me was really very shocking.

Eighteen months later Rob and I had finally saved up enough money for a deposit and we bought a house in Plumstead. As soon as we'd moved in, I threw myself into 'Operation Babymaking'. I still didn't feel like I really enjoyed having sex but if I wanted to get pregnant I knew it was something I had to do. But as the months passed and nothing happened, I became more and more convinced that I was infertile. I spent a fortune on sticks that I'd wee on every morning to check when I was ovulating and Rob and I started rowing about it.

'I feel so stressed all the time and Rob says I'm putting too much pressure on him,' I confided in Laraine.

'You'll be fine, Deb,' she told me. 'It will happen.'

'But how do you know?' I said. 'What if it doesn't?'

'You know Brendan and me had trouble because of my polycystic ovaries. It took us ages to have Jordan but we got there in the end.'

'I know, Lal,' I said. 'You were lucky but I'm just not convinced. I really think I can't have kids.'

A few weeks later, I was about to go back to the doctor and ask to be referred for tests when I realised that my period was a day late. I rushed out and bought a pregnancy test.

As I sat on the toilet and stared at the blue line appearing on the white plastic stick, I should have been ecstatic. My dreams had come true. The one thing that I'd wanted for so long was finally happening. But I just burst into tears.

I was overwhelmed with panic and I didn't feel like celebrating. I'd wanted to get pregnant to prove that I could, but now it was actually happening and it was real, I realised that I was terrified. What if I didn't love the baby? What if it was a girl and something happened to her and I couldn't keep her safe?

'I don't think I can do this,' I sobbed to Rob when I showed him the test.

'Don't be daft,' he said. 'You're going to make a brilliant mum. You'll see.'

I think he was just relieved that I was finally pregnant.

Slowly I started to get used to the idea of being a mother. But as my bump grew, it was replaced by another fear: I was petrified about giving birth and people examining me and poking and prodding me down below. As it turned out, I was too out of it to care.

I was in labour for three days at Greenwich hospital. I was in agony but I just wasn't progressing.

'You can start pushing now,' the midwife said finally.

For over an hour I gave it my best shot but nothing was happening and I was exhausted.

'I can't do this any more,' I cried. 'I'm shattered.'

'You can,' said Rob, squeezing my hand. 'Keep going, Deb.'

I pushed and pushed with all my might but then suddenly the midwife stopped me.

'No more pushing,' she said. 'I just need to call the doctor in to examine you.'

She pressed a button by the bed and suddenly all of these people appeared.

'What is it?' I said. 'Is my baby OK?'

I was terrified that something was really wrong.

'Your baby's almost here but it's stuck in the birth canal and your contractions have stopped,' the midwife explained. 'If you push now there's a risk your cervix could split and you might bleed to death.'

'Do what you need to,' I said. 'As long as my baby's OK.'

I knew they had to get the baby out quickly, so they gave me something to stimulate the contractions. Finally, with the help of a ventouse, they sucked her out.

'Here she is,' said the midwife. 'A beautiful baby girl.'

As she handed her to me, all my worries about having a daughter melted away. I loved her instantly. We decided to call her Victoria.

'I love you so much, little one,' I sobbed. 'I'm never going to let anyone hurt you.'

Rob was in pieces.

'It was horrible watching you go through all that,' he said. 'I thought I was going to lose both of you.'

He eventually went home to get some rest and a doctor came round to check on Vicky and me. There was a nurse with him and he pointed something out to her in my notes and she drew the curtains around my bed.

'Mrs Grafham, there's something I need to ask you,' he said.

'Yes?' I asked.

'Are you in an abusive relationship?'

'No, I am not,' I said, shocked. 'I've only been married a couple of years and my husband's the kindest man you could meet.'

'I see,' he said. 'Where is your husband now?'

'He's gone home to get some sleep as we've both been awake for three days. He'll be back later, though.'

He didn't say anything else and walked off. I was terrified. I remembered the midwife talking to me about some damage and scarring to my cervix when I'd been in labour but I'd been too out of it to understand. Maybe that was what he was referring to?

I started to panic. What if they mentioned to Rob

what they had found and said it was a sign I'd been abused? I was so scared that for a moment I wondered if I should tell him.

But thankfully nobody mentioned it again and I was so wrapped up in Vicky, I knew the moment had passed to confide in Rob.

Laraine came to see me in hospital.

'You've done so well, Deb,' she said. 'I'm so happy for you.'

I let her cuddle Vicky but Lal, Rob and Mum were the only ones that I trusted with my daughter.

As soon as I brought her home, I was determined to be a perfect mother. I was terrified of something happening to her, so I did everything by the book. I breastfed her, bathed her each day, changed her nappies every half an hour so they were never too wet. Friends and family came round to visit but I wouldn't let them pick her up or even touch her.

Rob's mum Shirley was round one day and Vicky was screaming her head off. I was trying to eat dinner with one hand and hold her in the other.

'Let me take her for you,' she said. 'I'll nurse her while you finish your food.'

'No,' I snapped. 'Don't touch her, I'm fine.'

I knew she thought I was being obsessively overprotective but there was no way that I was going to be parted from my baby.

Vicky was three months old when she had her second

lot of injections. She'd been fine after the first but this time when I brought her home from the doctor's, she just slept and slept for the next couple of days. I had to keep waking her up for a feed but she wasn't interested and she was burning hot.

I panicked and rang Rob at work.

'I think there's something wrong with Vicky,' I told him.

I got a taxi to take us to Greenwich hospital, where we were admitted to Accident and Emergency.

'How long has she been like this?' asked the doctor.

'Two days,' I said.

They did test after test but they couldn't work out what was wrong. I was hysterical.

'What if we lose her?' I sobbed to Rob.

Thankfully they ruled out meningitis but they said they needed a urine sample and as she wasn't weeing much, they would have to put a needle through her tummy and into her bladder. I couldn't bring myself to look.

'I can't bear to watch someone hurting my daughter,' I said to Rob.

I handed Vicky to him and ran outside in tears. Hours passed and Rob went home to get some sleep. As soon as he'd left, a doctor came to see me.

'Tests showed that your daughter has a urine infection,' he said.

'It's very rare for a baby that age to have something like that so I just need to ask you a few questions.'

'Of course,' I said.

'How often is she washed and bathed?'

'At least once a day,' I said. 'More if she's had a dirty nappy.'

'Have you ever left her alone with anyone else?'

'No,' I said. 'Only my mum and my husband.'

'Has anyone else who has ever been to the house been left with her?'

'No,' I said. 'I told you only Rob and my mum. Why are you asking me all these questions?'

'As I explained, it's very rare for a baby this young to have this type of infection and we need to try and find out why she's got it,' the doctor said.

Suddenly the penny dropped.

'You think someone's been touching her, don't you?' I gasped.

'I'm not saying that, Mrs Grafham,' said the doctor. 'But we need to rule out every possibility.'

I felt sick. It was like all my worst nightmares had come true. Even though I knew neither Mum nor Rob were capable of that it played on all my fears. I knew Mum would never do that to her own grandchild but for a split second I doubted Rob.

'We'll have to do further investigations and get back to you,' he said.

I couldn't believe this was happening. Rob had been left on his own with Vicky but only when I was in the bath. Even then I used to make him undress her and I'd bring her in the water with me.

I knew in my heart that he would never hurt our daughter and I felt sick that even a tiny part of me had suspected him. There were more tests and examinations and finally a different doctor came to see me.

'Your baby looks fine to me,' he said. 'She's obviously very well cared for and she has no obvious injuries.'

It was such a relief but I never ever dared tell Rob about what the doctors had said or my suspicions. I knew he would be devastated that I could even think that about him.

A few weeks later I went back to see our GP to get the test results from the hospital. It turned out that Vicky had bacteria growing in her bladder from one of her vaccinations. For some reason her body hadn't absorbed it and it had caused the infection.

'It really upset me what they were implying,' I told the doctor.

'It's very rare for such a tiny baby to get an infection like that,' she said. 'They have to look at every possibility.'

But little did she know how it had awakened all sorts of fears from my past. Every so often something like this would happen that would bring it all back.

Despite my worries, I loved being a mum and I quickly went on to have two other children – Louise was born when Vicky was two and she was followed two years later by a son, who we called Daniel. Laraine had another son too – a lovely little boy called Mitchell – and when he was a year old, she and Brendan finally got married. It was just a small wedding at the local register office.

We were all happy and settled, but it never lasted for long...

One day David came round and dropped a bombshell. 'Guess what?' he said excitedly. 'I've found our dad.'

'What?' I gasped.

It was such a shock even though David had talked about tracing Dad for years.

'I really want to find him,' he'd told me. 'I often think about him, don't you, Debbie?'

'No,' I'd said. 'I couldn't care less after the way he treated us.

'I want nothing more to do with him.'

I didn't ever think he was serious, but unbeknown to me he'd been to the Salvation Army and they'd traced Dad and put them in touch.

'He's got nowhere to live at the minute so I said he could stay with me for a while,' he told me.

Typical Dad, I thought. He obviously hadn't changed one bit.

David, Davina and Laraine were all excited to have him back in our lives but I was horrified.

'He wants to see you all,' he told me.

'I'm not interested,' I said.

The others couldn't understand why I was being so horrible.

'Why are you being so mean about him, Deb?' said Laraine.

'Have you forgotten all the bad times we went through as kids and how awful he was to Mum?' I asked her.

I'd certainly never forgotten what he'd done to me.

I couldn't believe it when Mum said she wanted to see him, too.

'Why?' I said. 'It's been twenty years since he was last in our lives and we're better off without him.'

'I'm just curious, I think,' she told me.

I could see she was nervous about it, though, and I didn't want her going on her own.

'Don't worry, I'll come with you for moral support,' I said.

David arranged for us to meet him one afternoon at The Standard pub in Blackheath. I dreaded seeing him again but I put on a brave face for Mum because I knew she was apprehensive.

When we walked in, I recognised him straight away. He was sitting at a table in the corner. Those twenty years had aged him and he didn't look very well. He seemed frail and his face was all gaunt. It was horrible seeing him again, remembering what he had done to me all those years ago. But at the same time he didn't scare me any more. How could I be frightened of this old man in his seventies?

'Nice to see you, Mo,' he said to Mum, giving her a kiss.

I hung back and didn't say a word.

'Well, Debbie,' he said to me. 'Are you going to forgive your old dad, then?'

'I've only come because Mum wanted to see you,' I said coldly.

He and Mum chatted for a while but I didn't ask him any questions. He told us how he'd been working away, drifting around the country. No doubt in and out of prison as usual.

'Debbie, I hear you're married and have got little ones,' he said. 'When can I meet Rob and the kids?'

I didn't say a word. I felt ill at the thought of him being anywhere near my children.

We only stayed an hour and I was relieved when we left. He and Mum had got on well and my worst fear was that she would let him back in her life. I couldn't bear the thought of that.

'I really hope you're not going to get back with him,' I told her.

'That's not going to happen, Debbie,' she said and she was adamant.

I really didn't want my father to meet Rob or the kids but everyone kept going on about it.

'He just wants to see his grandchildren, Deb,' Laraine told me. 'You can't deny him that.'

No one knew what he had done to me and even Rob was keen.

'Why don't we invite him over to us for Christmas?' he said.

Mum, David and Laraine were coming round and they all made me feel guilty that he was spending Christmas on his own.

'OK,' I said.

I told myself that it was just one day and after that I didn't have to have anything more to do with him. Rob knew that he hadn't been very nice to us when we were younger but he didn't know to what extent and there was no way I was going to tell him. I didn't want Dad to ruin this good part of my life. I was hoping that my father would see the children once and then would soon lose interest. When he came round on Christmas Day, I was completely on edge. I watched him like a hawk and I made sure I never left him alone in the room with any of the children.

Vicky was four by then and like me, she loved animals and was obsessed with getting a pet.

'I really want a doggy,' she said. 'Please can we get one, Mummy?'

'Don't worry, sweetheart, Granddad will get you a puppy,' my dad piped up.

His words sent a chill down my spine as I remembered Judy and the night that he'd brought her home for me.

Thankfully, we got through Christmas. Dad moved to a flat in Charlton and even though he often rang and asked to come round, I always made excuses.

One day in the New Year, David had given me a lift to the shops.

'I know, Debbie, why don't we call in and see Dad on the way home?' he said. 'He'd really like to see you.'

'No thanks,' I said. 'Just drop me home.'

But David and I started to argue about it and he got really cross.

'I think you're being really unfair, Deb,' he yelled. 'Why don't you go and visit Dad and let the kids see more of him? He is their granddad.'

He kept going on and on about it, saying how unreasonable I was being.

'I don't understand it,' said David. 'What's your bloody problem with him? Why don't you ever want to see him?'

I'd had enough.

'Because he raped me, that's why,' I yelled.

David's face fell.

'He did *what*?' he gasped.

'He raped me, David. One night when I was nine.'

'I'm going to kill the bastard,' he told me.

He obviously believed every word I'd said and I could see how angry he was. He put his foot down on the accelerator of his Ford Granada and we screeched off the road into a disused builder's yard.

'David, what are you playing at?' I said.

I was terrified about what he was going to do.

'The dirty bastard,' he said, shaking his head. 'I can't believe he did that to you.'

'I didn't mean it,' I said. 'It's not true about Dad, David. I was making it up.'

'I can tell by your face that you're telling the truth,' he said.

He was absolutely livid. Suddenly he put his foot down on the accelerator and we screeched down a dead end.

'David!' I screamed. 'What the hell are you doing?'

Then there was a massive bang and we both lurched forward as he drove into a brick wall.

'You're crazy,' I said. 'You could have killed us.'

The car was a wreck and we were shaken up, but thankfully we were both OK.

'Why didn't you tell me, Deb? Before I brought him back into all our lives.'

'I couldn't,' I said. 'You're the only one who knows.'

When he'd finally calmed down we got the bus home.

That night I couldn't sleep as I was so worried about David. He'd been so angry when I'd told him about Dad and I was worried that he was going to do something stupid.

I didn't say anything to anyone but next morning I dropped the kids at Mum's and went round to see David. I banged and banged on the door of his flat but there was no one there.

I knew instantly where he was. Dad lived just around the corner from him, so I went round to his flat.

Please don't let him have done anything stupid, I prayed.

David could be a bit of a loose cannon sometimes and I'd never seen him so angry.

The front door to Dad's flat was open and I was shaking with nerves as I walked in.

'Dad?' I shouted. 'David?'

'In here,' said a voice.

I walked into the living room to find David sat on the sofa. Then I saw the shotgun in his hand.

'What have you got that for?' I gasped. 'Where's Dad?'

'I came round to kill him but he's not here,' said David.

'Don't be silly. Just put the gun down.'

'No,' he said. 'He deserves to die for what he did to you.'

'David, give the gun to me or I'm going to call the police,' I urged him.

But he shook his head. So I picked up my mobile and started dialling.

'OK, OK,' he said suddenly, getting up and handing me the gun.

I was terrified. We got in the car and drove to the Thames.

I gave the gun to David.

'Now get out and throw it into the river,' I said.

I was so relieved when he did as I'd asked and got back in the car.

By a complete coincidence, Dad had done one of his disappearing acts again. He didn't come back to the flat that day and none of us ever saw him again. Little did he know that doing a runner had probably saved his life.

'I don't want anything more to do with that bastard,' David told me.

Thankfully he promised not to tell anyone about what had happened. It made me even more sure never to tell anyone about Patrick Ryan. Bad things happened when secrets came out. More than ever I was determined that my past was going to remain well and truly hidden.

Chapter 12

Haunted by the Past

As the kids got older, we started to want a change of scene.

'I'd love to live by the sea,' said Rob.

So we looked at Margate, Weston-super-Mare and finally settled on Eastbourne. I was all for it as I wanted to get as far away as possible from southeast London and the past. But the rest of my family was upset about us moving.

'I don't want you to go, Deb,' said Laraine. 'I'm really gonna miss you.'

'We're only an hour away on the train and I'll call you every day,' I told her.

David wasn't happy about it either, especially when, a few months later, Mum decided to move down to be near us. I'd got a new job as a care assistant at Eastbourne General Hospital and she offered to look after the kids while I went back to work. She was looking forward to a new start as well, but there was one thing on her mind.

'I'm really worried about David,' she told me. 'I don't like leaving him up there in London. He's drinking a lot these days.'

'He's always liked a drink, Mum,' I replied.

'But in these past few years since his marriage broke up he's really hit the booze,' she said. 'I don't think I've seen him without a can of Tennent's in his hand.'

I felt guilty as since we'd moved I hadn't had much chance to visit him. We hadn't even seen him at Christmas as he'd said he couldn't afford to come down.

Every New Year's Eve David phoned and this year it was no exception. I could tell he was drunk when he rang, but if there was one night of the year when most people were sozzled, this was it.

'Debbie, I'm not very well,' he said. 'Will you come up and see me tomorrow?'

It didn't sound like my happy-go-lucky brother and I was worried.

'If you're not well, David, then you need to see a doctor,' I told him.

'I ain't going to no doctor, Deb.'

I explained that I wanted to see him but that I was working the next day, on New Year's Day.

'How about I come the day after?' I said. 'I'll get the train up on the second.'

'OK,' he said. 'But if you don't come up, will you promise me one thing?'

'You know I will,' I told him. 'What?'

'Will you tell the police about the abuse with the foster parents and what Dad did to you?'

I was taken aback as we'd never ever spoken about Auntie and Uncle before.

'Do you remember what they did to us, Debbie?' he asked.

'Of course I do,' I said. 'You don't ever forget something like that.'

'Me neither. I often think about the awful things those sick bastards put us through but as a bloke, I find it really hard to talk about. I've never got over it, you know.'

Poor David. Why had he never told me any of this before?

'Please, Debbie,' he slurred. 'Promise me that you'll report them. That you'll tell someone what they did to us.'

'OK,' I said. 'I promise you. There's something else I need to tell you too, David.'

'What?' he slurred.

'Remember when we lived at Coleraine Road and there was that man upstairs?'

'You mean that bloke Pat?' he said. 'Michael and Shayne's dad?'

'Yeah, that's the one,' I told him. 'I've never told anyone this before but when we lived there he abused me. He raped me, David.'

The line went silent. David didn't say a word.

'I don't believe this, Debbie,' he sighed. 'Why didn't you tell me before? Why didn't you tell Mum?'

'Because he threatened to kill me, that's why. I was so scared, David.'

'You've got to tell the police about what's happened

to you, Debbie,' he told me. 'Otherwise it will get you in the end, just like it's got me.

'Do you promise me?'

'I promise you, David,' I said. 'Now go to bed, you sound drunk.'

'OK, Sis,' he replied. 'I do love you, you know.'

'I know you do, David. I'll phone you tomorrow and see you the day after that. You go and get some sleep.'

I'd never heard him like that before but I could tell he was drunk.

He won't remember a single word of what he said to me in the morning, I thought. He'll forget all about it.

That suited me. The last thing I wanted was for the past to be dragged back up. I didn't want to go to the police about the foster parents and Patrick Ryan. Who was going to believe us now after all these years?

The next day I went to work as normal. I was going to phone David to see how he was feeling but I didn't get home until late.

I'll call him in the morning, I decided. But at 8am the next day my mobile rang. It was his girlfriend, Emma.

'It's David,' she said. 'He's not well.'

I could hear the panic in her voice.

'What do you mean by not well?' I asked.

'He's on the floor and he won't get up. He's a funny yellow colour, Debbie, and there's brown stuff coming out of his mouth.'

I knew straight away that it was serious.

'Emma, you need to phone an ambulance right now,' I told her. 'Stay on the mobile with me and call 999 from the landline.'

She did as I said and I could hear her on the phone to the emergency services. Five minutes later I heard the rap on the door as the paramedics arrived.

'What's happening, Emma?' I asked. 'What are they doing?'

'It's OK, Debbie,' she said. 'He's in the back of the ambulance now and they're working on him.'

Having had some medical training through my job, I knew that wasn't a good sign otherwise they would have just driven him straight to hospital. Then suddenly I heard Emma gasp.

'Oh, God!' she said.

'Emma, what is it?' I yelled. 'Talk to me! What's happening?'

Then the line went dead.

I paced up and down the living room, ringing Emma's mobile over and over again but there was no answer. I decided to phone Mum.

'David's really ill,' I said. 'He's been taken to hospital in an ambulance but I can't get hold of Emma to find out what's going on.'

She was as worried as me. Then I phoned Laraine and told her the same thing. I'd just ended the call to her, when my mobile rang. It was Emma.

'How is he?' I said. 'What's happening?'

'Debbie, a doctor just phoned me. He was dead on arrival at Queen Elizabeth hospital.'

'Dead?' I said.

Her words didn't sink in. My brother couldn't be dead: he was only thirty-nine.

'They don't know what happened until they do a post-mortem but they think he was bleeding internally,' she said.

It was such a shock, I went into autopilot.

I rang Rob at work and said, 'David's dead.'

Then I phoned my work and told them, 'I won't be in today because my brother's just died but I'll be back tomorrow.'

I was numb. I couldn't bear the thought of telling Mum, so Rob offered to go round and see her.

Then Laraine phoned me. She'd just spoken to Emma and could barely speak for crying.

'I can't believe he's gone, Deb, and we'll never see him again,' she sobbed.

We were all devastated.

The post-mortem results showed that David had a perforated duodenal ulcer which had haemorrhaged, and cirrhosis of the liver; both were caused by alcohol abuse. He'd been bleeding internally for quite a while and must have been in agony but Emma said he'd refused to see a doctor. I knew he liked a drink but I hadn't realised to what extent. None of us had had any idea of how seriously ill he was.

I went to pieces. I felt so guilty that I hadn't gone to visit him and that I hadn't ever tried to talk to him about the abuse we'd suffered.

I went to see him at the chapel of rest. I put a chain and cross around his neck and cut off a lock of his dark curly hair.

'I'm so sorry, David,' I told him. 'I should have been there for you. I was so wrapped up in my own problems, I didn't know what you were going through.'

At his funeral at Charlton cemetery, I insisted on helping to carry his coffin into the chapel.

I blamed myself. He'd obviously found the foster parents' abuse really hard to cope with. Instead of drinking himself to death, why hadn't we talked about it? Perhaps I could have helped? I knew more than anyone how something like that could eat away at you for years.

In the weeks after David's death, I did something stupid, considering what had happened to him – I hit the bottle. I'd never been a big drinker. I liked a couple of glasses of wine but only if I was out and I never drank at home. But I started coming in from work and opening a bottle of wine. All day I would look forward to getting home and taking that first gulp of white wine.

'Do you fancy a glass?' I'd ask Rob.

But he didn't drink so I'd end up finishing the whole bottle. I liked the way it made my head feel fuzzy and stopped me from thinking about what had happened.

Then after a while, I'd get through one bottle so quickly that I would open another one and finish that off as well. It got to be a habit and before I knew it, it was out of control.

I was having trouble sleeping too so I'd sit up most of the night, drinking and thinking about what David had said to me. Despite my promise to him, I really didn't want to tell anyone about what the foster parents had done to us. What good would it do now? I couldn't put myself through that but I felt so guilty as it was the one thing David had asked me to do.

I didn't want Rob to know how much I was drinking. I'd hide the empties in the normal rubbish rather than the recycling bin so that he couldn't tell how much wine I was getting through.

He knew something wasn't right, though. I think he put it down to grief at first but then as the months passed, he started to suspect what I was doing.

He saw the state of me one morning. I knew I couldn't go to work at the hospital because I was still drunk.

'You look terrible,' he said.

'I'm so tired, Rob,' I told him. 'I was up half the night. I don't think I can go to work.'

'You're drunk, more like,' he said. 'I'm not stupid, Debbie. I can still smell the booze on your breath – I know how much wine you're getting through.'

I didn't say anything; I just felt so ashamed.

'Why are you doing this to yourself?' he said. 'If

you're not careful you're going to end up like that alkie brother of yours.'

Even though I knew Rob had my best interests at heart, I was furious.

'My brother wasn't just some pisshead,' I shouted. 'People have a reason why they drink too much! You don't know what he was going through.'

'And what was that then?' asked Rob.

Before I could think about what I was saying, it all came tumbling out. I told him about being sent to the foster parents after Mum's breakdown and how David was abused every single night for months.

'I didn't realise how much it had affected him,' I said. 'I don't think he ever got over it.'

I could tell by Rob's face that he was shocked and I knew exactly what he was going to say next.

'It happened to you too, Debbie, didn't it?' he said.

My eyes filled with tears. I felt so ashamed, I couldn't even look at him.

'Yes,' I nodded.

Rob came over and put his arms around me.

'Oh, Deb,' he said. 'I always knew there was something but I didn't want to come out and ask you in case I'd got it horribly wrong. Why didn't you tell me?'

'Because I didn't think you'd want anything to do with me,' I sobbed.

At first it felt like a relief to tell someone after all these years. But then, when I'd sobered up, I instantly regretted blurting it out. It was too late, though; the wheels were already in motion. That day Rob phoned a helpline for victims of child abuse.

'They said you should think about going to the police,' he told me.

'I don't want to go to the police,' I said. 'They won't believe me and even if they did, they're not going to do anything about it now.

'I was four years old, for God's sake! I'm not even sure of their surname, never mind their address.'

'Debbie, you've got to,' he said. 'You told me it's what David wanted.'

That was the only reason that I agreed to go through with it. I'd wrestled with my conscience for months about breaking the promise that I'd made him but now it was out of my hands. I couldn't even bring myself to listen when Rob made the call to Eastbourne Police.

'An officer's coming round tomorrow to take a statement,' he said. 'I'll have the day off work so I can be here when they come.'

I was dreading it. That night I didn't sleep a wink, I just sat up, drinking wine. At 9am a police officer was on the doorstep. It was a bloke in his thirties and he seemed nice enough but I was dreading having to describe what I'd been through, especially to a man.

'I don't know why I'm bothering. I know you probably won't believe me,' I said.

'Mrs Grafham, I'm sure you're telling the truth. I

just need to ask you a few questions and I'll take down some information,' he said.

Rob sat with me on the sofa as I described what Auntie and Uncle had done to us. My hands gripped a mug filled with tea but I desperately wished that it was wine in there instead.

'I know it's difficult but I need to know exactly how they touched you,' he said.

I felt so embarrassed, describing the things that had happened to David and I. My voice was barely a whisper as I told him about the bedtime stories and the touching. I couldn't look at him or Rob, I was mortified.

'Is this the first time you've talked about it?' the officer asked, writing everything down.

'Yes,' I said. 'But I can remember everything. I can tell you exactly how that house looked, down to the Paisley carpet on the stairs.'

I was determined not to cry but I couldn't stop myself when I had to describe what they'd done to David.

'He died last year,' I sobbed. 'He never got over what they did to him.'

After two exhausting hours of questions, it was finally over. My hands were shaking and I was desperate for a drink. I just wanted the policeman to go so I could have some wine and try and blot out those memories.

'You did so well, Deb,' Rob told me afterwards.

But I was a wreck. It made me even more sure that I could never tell anyone about Patrick Ryan and what he had done. I couldn't cope with going through that all again.

'It's over now,' I said. 'I did what David wanted and now it's in the hands of the police.'

But one thing I did know was that after going through the trauma of making a statement, I wanted the police to find the foster parents. I wanted to make them pay for what they'd done to David and I, all those years ago. He wasn't here to back up my story but at last I had kept my promise to him.

'I'm doing this for you, David,' I said as I took my first gulp of white wine.

I didn't tell my mum or Laraine. I was still so ashamed that I couldn't bear another person knowing.

But a few weeks later the police officer phoned me.

'It's not good news, I'm afraid,' he said.

He explained that they'd tried their best but they were unable to trace the foster parents based on the details that I had given them and there were no Social Service records available.

'So I'm afraid we're unable to pursue it any further,' he said.

It was a huge blow. I was angry, upset, disappointed and maybe at the same time slightly relieved.

'I put myself through all that for nothing,' I sobbed to Rob.

It had opened up old wounds for no reason and I took it badly. I was drinking more and more, and took so many sick days off from work. But slowly, over time, I started to come to terms with the fact that nothing could be done.

One day I went to David's grave in Charlton cemetery, where he was buried alongside Granddad George.

'I'm so sorry, David,' I said. 'I did my best. I kept my promise but they've got away with it. I hope you can rest in peace now.'

I knew there was nothing more that could be done and I just had to accept it. It made me even more sure that I could never tell anyone about Patrick Ryan or my father. I wasn't going to put myself through that again and it come to nothing.

In time, I managed to cut down on my drinking and slowly I got back on track. But I was never allowed to forget the past for too long. One day Davina called.

'I've got some bad news,' she said. 'Dad's dead.'

Someone was trying to trace his relatives and had found her name and phone number at the back of one of his diaries. She explained that he'd had lung cancer and had passed away a couple of weeks ago.

'I feel so bad none of us were there with him,' she told me.

'I don't,' I said. 'I'm glad he's dead.'

'Oh, Debbie, you always were so horrible about him!'

I knew she was shocked but I didn't care. All I felt was relief.

Mum didn't really have any feelings for him any more

either. I think over time she'd come to hate him and wish that she'd left him sooner, but Davina and Laraine were upset. They were the only ones crying at his funeral while I stood there, stony-faced. I'd only gone to prove to myself that he was really dead.

Dad had always been good at drawing and when the priest was paying tribute to him he said, 'We'll always remember Fred because he was very artistic with his hands.'

Before I could stop myself, I burst out laughing.

'*Deb*!' said Laraine.

I knew only too well how artistic he was with those hands of his.

None of the others knew what I was laughing about, of course. I think they thought I was just being a bit weird.

It was a long, drawn-out Catholic service and I was glad when it was over. As we all got up and walked out of the chapel, I turned around to take one last look at him. I watched the velvet curtains close on Dad's coffin before it was cremated and all I felt was a huge sense of relief. The past could stay in the past now as far as I was concerned. Little did I know what was about to happen.

Chapter 13

Allegations and Revelations

Picking up my mobile, I dialled the number for what felt like the hundredth time that day.

'Come on, Lal,' I said out loud, drumming my fingers on the kitchen table. 'Answer your bloody phone for God's sake!'

Now that I lived fifty miles away, I couldn't just pop in and see my little sister and I was really worried about her. Mum had gone up to London the other week and had come back really concerned.

'Laraine looks terrible,' she said. 'She's drinking way too much.'

I had a horrible sense of déjà vu after everything we'd been through with David. I know I'd had my own issues with booze in the past too, but I was determined not to lose another loved one to alcohol.

Even though I didn't see her that often, Laraine and I would talk every day. We'd chat on the phone, we'd post silly things to each other on Facebook or she'd text me.

Hi Lal. Miss ya! What you up to? xx

Miss u 2 Deb. Come and see u soon x

But today I'd not heard a peep from her, which I thought was strange. As the day went on, I grew more and more concerned. Just before tea time someone finally answered the phone.

'Thank God, Lal, I was getting worried about you,' I said.

'It's not Laraine, it's Mitchell,' said a boy's voice.

'Oh hello,' I said. 'It's Auntie Debbie here. I've been ringing all day, trying to get hold of your mum.

'Has she gone shopping?'

'No, I think she's poorly,' he said. 'She's on the floor and she can't get up.'

I knew then Mum was right, things had got really bad.

'Listen, Mitchell, don't worry,' I told him. 'I'll call your dad at work and get him to come home.'

I rang Brendan at the garage where he was a mechanic and he went straight back to their bungalow in Erith.

'She's in a right state, Debbie,' he told me. 'She's been on the red wine again. As soon as I go to work, she goes out and gets it. I don't know what to do.'

I was really concerned. The next day I phoned her up and she sounded dreadful.

'You can't go on like this,' I told her. 'You're going to kill yourself, like David. You need to go to hospital and dry out.'

'I don't want to go to hospital,' she said. 'I'm fine.'

But every time I spoke to Laraine, I could tell she

was drunk. She'd be slurring her words and crying down the phone.

'I made dinner but it turned out all wrong,' she slurred. 'It's all burnt and black.'

'I'm not surprised, Lal, you're pissed. You shouldn't be anywhere near a cooker in that state.'

I was constantly worried she was going to burn the house down or hurt herself. I had to call an ambulance one day when Mitchell rang me and said she'd fallen over and banged her head, but she refused to go to hospital.

Brendan and Jordan were out at work all day and Mitchell was at school so there was no one around to stop her from buying alcohol. I knew there was only one thing for it: I would have to go up there and take her to hospital myself.

Davina and I got the train up to London and went round to Laraine's. We hadn't told her we were coming and when she opened the door to us, I was shocked.

'Oh, Lal,' I said. 'What have you done to yourself?'

She looked awful. It'd been a couple of months since I'd seen her last and the whites of her eyes were yellow, her skin all red and blotchy. She'd always been quite curvy but she'd lost so much weight, her clothes were hanging off her.

It wasn't even 11am and she was already drunk. The house was a tip and there were piles of washing up and a couple of empty wine bottles on the side. I'd never seen her like that before and it was frightening.

'We need to get you to hospital,' I told her. 'I don't want to lose you.'

I phoned St Mary's in Sidcup, where I knew they had a detox unit, and they agreed we could bring her in.

'We're going to call a cab and take you to hospital,' I told her.

But she was so out of it, she wasn't making any sense and she could barely walk.

'I don't think she even knows what day it is,' said Davina.

It was devastating to see my little sister like that and it was such a relief when they admitted her. At least I knew she was in a safe place now and getting the help she needed.

I went to see her every week and slowly, as the effects of the alcohol wore off, she started to look better. The doctors said her liver was slightly enlarged but that hopefully it would repair itself if she stayed off the booze. She started to seem like the old Laraine again.

'Thank you for being there for me, Deb, and making me see sense,' she told me. 'I don't know what I'd do without you.'

'You did this,' I said. 'You got yourself through detox. Now you've got to be strong and make sure you stay away from the drink.'

She was having sessions with a social worker called Antoinette to talk about how she was going to cope when she went back home. During one of my visits, Antoinette took me to one side.

'I know Laraine's been through a lot and her memory is a bit patchy because of the extent of her drinking. But I thought I should let you know that she's been making allegations of child abuse.'

I paused for a minute, trying to take in what she'd just said.

'What do you mean?' I asked. 'What's she told you?'

'She's been talking about being raped by a man called Patrick.'

I felt sick at the mention of his name.

'Do you know him?' she asked. 'Is he a family member?'

'No, he's an old neighbour of ours,' I told her. 'My sister's very confused at the minute. Let me have a talk to her.'

I couldn't believe what I was hearing. Why, after all this time, had Laraine said something about Patrick Ryan? We'd never ever discussed what had happened. Why had she chosen to open up this can of worms now?

As soon as I sat down next to her bed, she brought it up.

'Deb, I've decided I really want to tell someone,' she said.

'Tell someone about what?' I asked.

'About that Patrick Ryan and what he did to me. I haven't forgotten and I need to get it off my chest.

'You remember him, don't you, Deb? He had long hair and a ponytail and I fell down the stairs. I remember you trying to get him off me.

'You know what he did, you were there.'

'Of course I do,' I said. 'I'm not going to forget that in a hurry.

'But why now, Lal? Why say something now after all these years? You've been through so much already.'

This was the first time that she had ever talked to me about the abuse.

'I've always had what he did to me at the back of my mind,' she said. 'I was drinking to try and blot it out. I know no one's going to believe me but I want to tell someone.'

'You've been through so much,' I told her. 'You need to focus on getting better rather than talking to the police about something that happened thirty-odd years ago.'

'I suppose you're right,' she said.

I prayed that was an end to it. I just wanted the whole thing forgotten.

After three months Laraine came out of hospital. She was still weak but she looked a million times better.

'Now remember what the doctors said and make sure you stay off the booze,' I told her. 'I promise I'll come and see you every week.'

'Yes, Deb,' she said. 'Don't worry, I've learned my lesson.'

I hadn't mentioned Patrick Ryan since. I was hoping that she'd forgotten what she'd said to me while she was in hospital or changed her mind. But when I went to see her at home, she started talking about it again. To my horror, she seemed more determined than ever to go to the police.

'I just want to tell someone even though I know they probably won't believe me.

'What do you think I should do?' she asked me.

Really I thought she should keep her mouth well and truly shut. I didn't want her to say anything because I knew I would be dragged into it and I didn't want anyone to know what I'd been through. It had been thirty-three years since Patrick Ryan had last abused us when we'd left Coleraine Road.

'It's up to you,' I said. 'But I don't want to be involved.'

'Why not, Deb?' she said. 'You're the only one who saw him. You know what he did to me.'

'If you want to call the police then do it, but please keep me out of it.'

Five months after coming out of hospital, Laraine phoned me one morning.

'I finally did it,' she said. 'I called the police and told them about Ryan. They're coming round in a couple of hours to take a statement.'

She didn't want to speak to them until Brendan and Jordan were at work and Mitchell was at school as she hadn't told any of them about the abuse.

I really hadn't thought she would go through with it and I was terrified. It felt like things were spiralling out of control and I knew it was just a matter of time before the police contacted me.

Sure enough, later that day I got a call from an unknown number.

'Mrs Grafham?'

'Yes.'

'This is PC Carol Day from the Sapphire Unit in Sidcup,' she said. 'Your sister Laraine has made an allegation of historic child abuse against an old neighbour of yours called Patrick Ryan. She says that you witnessed the abuse and we'd like to speak to you about it.'

I didn't say a word. My heart was racing.

'Mrs Grafham, please could we come round and see you as we'd like to take a witness statement?'

It was my worst nightmare come true.

'No, thank you,' I said. 'Like I told Laraine, I don't want to be involved in any way.'

'Perhaps we could just come down to Eastbourne and talk to you? You see you're the only person who can verify your sister's story.'

'No way.' I told her. 'I'm not doing it. I'm not interested.'

Then I hung up.

Over the next few days she kept ringing me but I didn't answer it. I knew I could only put her off for so long. I started drinking heavily again to try and forget what was happening, but I couldn't hide from the past any more.

One night Rob got home from work to find me sprawled out on the sofa, drunk.

'Debbie, this has got to stop,' he said. 'What is it? Why are you drinking so much again?'

He looked so worried it broke my heart.

'Laraine's been to the police about something that happened when we were kids,' I said.

I told him about Patrick Ryan and how I had caught him abusing Laraine.

'She wants me to talk to the police and give them a witness statement, but I really don't want to.'

'Why not?' he asked. 'Poor Laraine, going through all that. If you saw him then I don't understand why you wouldn't want to back up your own sister.'

I turned away, I couldn't look at him. And then he just knew.

'He did it to you too, didn't he?'

'Yes,' I said, my voice almost a whisper.

Rob was shocked and I'd never seen him so angry before.

'What did that sick bastard do?' he said.

'He raped and humiliated me over three years,' I said. 'And then there was my father, too.'

He was horrified.

'For Christ's sake, Debbie, why didn't you tell me this before?' he said. 'I could have helped you. Tried to make it better.'

'No one could, Rob,' I said. 'I was just so ashamed and disgusted at myself. Laraine doesn't even know what Ryan did to me.'

'I'm just upset that you didn't feel like you trusted me enough to tell me,' he said.

'Of course I trust you,' I sobbed. 'I was just so scared of losing you. Then as the years passed, there was never a right time.'

I knew more than anyone the longer that you kept something a secret, the harder it was to tell.

'You've got to tell Laraine that he abused you, too,' Rob told me.

'I can't,' I said. 'I don't want her to know. I'm worried that she'll start drinking again and that could kill her.'

I was dead against telling her even though it caused no end of arguments between us. Laraine couldn't understand why I wouldn't talk to the police and back her up.

'The police have just phoned me and said that you're refusing to speak to them or answer their calls,' she told me over the phone one day. 'I don't understand it, Deb. Why don't you believe me? Why don't you believe what he done?'

'Laraine, I do believe you,' I said. 'You know I do.'

'Well, then why can't you make this statement? I'm not asking you to lie. Just tell the police what you saw.'

'I just can't,' I said. 'I'm really busy at work at the minute and I can't have any time off to go to the police station. They've got your statement, that will have to do.'

Understandably, she was really upset and cross with me, but I was too scared to talk to the police. When I'd made a statement about the foster parents I had gone through all that, and for what? Absolutely nothing. I couldn't put myself through that trauma again. I didn't want to have to sit there and tell everyone what that man had done to me. I was still so ashamed and disgusted, I didn't even want my own sister to know. No way, I wasn't going to go through all of that for them to say that he was dead or they couldn't find him.

'I'm not prepared to make a statement,' I told PC Day when she next phoned. 'But if you come back to me and say that you've managed to trace Patrick Ryan, then perhaps I'll think again.'

That will put them off for a while, I thought.

I didn't think there was much hope of them being able to find him.

How wrong I was. Two months after Laraine had made her statement, she phoned me.

'They've got him, Deb,' she said. 'Can you believe it?'

'Got who?' I asked.

'Ryan. They found him. They arrested him yesterday and questioned him and now he's been released on bail.'

I was stunned to say the least. I just wanted it all to go away.

The police started phoning me again, asking me to make a statement. I knew they were just doing their job but I felt hounded, like things were spiralling out of my control.

A couple of days later DC Joanne Crockford called me.

'As you now know, Mr Ryan has been arrested and the bottom line is we need a witness statement,' she said. 'We need you to say what you saw, Mrs Grafham. You've been giving us the run-around for long enough.'

'OK,' I told her. 'If that means you lot will leave me alone then I'll do it. I'm coming up to London next week and you can have your bloody witness statement.'

I'd got tickets for me, Vicky and Louise to go and see Rihanna at the O2. We'd arranged to stay the night with Rob's dad in Charlton, so I had time in the day before the concert to go and talk to the police. Eddie met us at the station and he picked the girls up while I arranged to meet PC Carol Day there.

I'd come up with a plan. I would tell her exactly what I'd seen Patrick Ryan doing to Laraine but not mention what he'd done to me. That way I was backing up her story and hopefully they'd leave me alone.

But as I stood outside Charlton station waiting for her, I felt sick. Just the thought of having to talk about him again made me feel ill.

Thankfully, Carol seemed like a nice woman. She was in plain clothes and she showed me her card.

'I'm going to interview you at Plumstead police station,' she said.

We drove there in silence, my mind whirring. I was a bag of nerves.

Just say what you saw and leave it at that, I told myself over and over again. Don't think about what he did to you.

At the police station, Carol led me into an interview room. It was small and drab with stark beige walls and the only furniture in there was a desk and two plastic chairs.

'Right then, Debbie, let's get started,' she said. 'Your sister Laraine has told us about the abuse she was subjected to by Patrick Ryan but unfortunately it's very unlikely that it will go to court given the amount of time that has passed since it happened and the lack of forensic evidence.'

Good, I thought to myself.

'On its own Laraine's statement isn't strong enough to secure a prosecution. That's why we wanted to talk to you about what you witnessed.'

'I'm happy to tell you what I saw,' I said.

So I told her exactly what had happened and she wrote it all down. How I'd gone to the upstairs flat and found him abusing Laraine.

'Your sister seems confused about a few things,' she said. 'Because of her drinking her memory is very sketchy and there are some details that she's not clear on. How can you be sure these allegations are true?'

'They are true,' I said. 'I saw him.'

'These are serious allegations, Debbie. We have to be sure that everyone is telling the truth.'

'We are,' I said. 'I know he did it.'

I was getting really rattled by now. Why did they not believe my sister? She was telling the truth about what that bastard had done to her. Did they think I was making it up just to back Laraine up?

'I'm going to ask you one last time,' Carol said. 'How do you know that she's not imagined it?'

My heart was thumping out of my chest, my head was spinning and suddenly I felt like those four drab walls were starting to close in on me.

'How can you be so sure that it happened, Debbie?'

'Because he raped me, too,' I said.

Then I got up and walked out, horrified that after all these years I'd finally told my secret.

Chapter 14
The Truth

I ran out of the room and into the corridor. My head was spinning and I thought I was going to be sick. I couldn't breathe and I had to lean against a wall to stop myself from collapsing.

Oh God, why had I said that? What had I done?

Carol came running out after me.

'Debbie, I need you to come back into the interview room,' she said gently.

My hands were shaking as I sat back down on the plastic chair.

'What happens now?' I said. 'Now that I've told you he did it to me, too.'

'We need to finish the witness statement about what you saw with Laraine,' she said. 'Then at some point if you want to, I'd like you to make a separate statement about what Patrick Ryan did to you. Do you think you can do that, Debbie?'

'I don't know,' I said. 'I didn't want any of this to happen.'

What if, like with the foster parents, nothing came of it? Why should I put myself through that?

But I didn't feel like I had a choice any more.

'I will say this,' said Carol. 'With Laraine's statement it's very unlikely that the CPS will feel there's enough evidence to take it any further. It happened so many years ago and there's no forensic evidence. But if you make a statement too then it gives us a much better chance of it going to court and trying to secure a conviction.'

'I'm just not sure I can do it,' I said.

I went back to my father-in-law's in a daze. I'd told Eddie that I needed to speak to the police about a complaint Laraine had made but I hadn't told him any of the details.

'All sorted now,' I said, plastering a fake smile on my face.

But that couldn't have been any further from the truth. My head was all over the place and I couldn't enjoy the concert that night. All I kept thinking about was what I'd said to the police.

I was going to have to tell Laraine and Mum, and even my poor kids would have to know. If I made my own statement then everyone would know what Patrick Ryan had done to me.

I still wasn't sure I wanted to take it any further. I ignored any calls from officers at the Sapphire Unit. Then one day a police officer from Eastbourne rang and caught me by surprise.

'They thought it might be more convenient for you to speak to a local person,' an officer told me. 'We can come round to see you at home and you can make a statement to us and we'll pass it onto the Sapphire Unit.'

'I'll think about it,' I said. 'It's tricky with my husband and children around.'

They rang every few days, so to shut them up, I kept making appointments to go to the police station to be interviewed. But then when it came to it I just wouldn't show up. I was still drinking heavily and getting more and more paranoid. Every time a police car drove by I would be filled with dread, wondering if they were coming for me.

Meanwhile, Rob was getting increasingly worried.

'Debbie, if you don't say anything they might be able to arrest you for perverting the course of justice or something. Do you really want that to happen?'

Two months after I'd made my statement about Laraine, I couldn't take it any more.

'I'll give them their bloody statement then, seeing as that's all anybody wants,' I told Rob.

'Do you want me to come with you for moral support?' he asked.

'No,' I said. 'I'll go on my own.'

I couldn't bear the thought of him hearing in detail the sick, depraved things Patrick Ryan had put me through. I didn't want to bring that into my house or anywhere near my husband and children. So I arranged to be interviewed at Marlowe House in Sidcup, where the Sapphire Unit is based.

On the day of my appointment, I stood outside the huge tower block and it felt like I was rooted to the spot. I just knew I couldn't go through with it.

I'd worked myself up into such a state that I went into the pub opposite and ordered a bottle of white wine. I sat there for hours.

'I can't do this,' I told myself.

I phoned Karen Brown, the officer who was due to take my statement, but she'd been called out on a job.

'I'm going home,' I slurred. 'I ain't doing this.'

'Please don't, Debbie,' she said. 'Can you come back at 8am tomorrow and I'll be there waiting for you?'

'I don't think so,' I said.

I'd already arranged to spend the night at Laraine's. As soon as I got there I could tell she was drunk. I was furious as well as desperately worried.

'You're paralytic,' I said. 'How could you do that? You know the doctors said how dangerous it would be for you to start drinking again.'

She said that someone had bought her a bottle of wine for her birthday so she'd drunk it. I was so cross with her after going through all of that detox for nothing. I knew it was a bit hypocritical of me seeing as I'd spent most of the day in the pub, but I knew because of her heavy drinking in the past that Laraine's body wouldn't be able to cope with the strain.

'Why are you up here, anyway?' she slurred. 'I thought you'd already spoke to the police?'

'They just had a few more questions about my witness statement,' I replied. 'Nothing to worry about, Lal.'

There was no way I was going to tell her what was really going on when she was in this state. I was already concerned enough about her.

Before long she had passed out but I stayed up all night worrying. About Laraine and her drinking, about the statement, about everyone knowing about the sick things Ryan had done to us both.

Earlier that night I'd phoned my counsellor Lorna to tell her what was going on. I'd been having counselling ever since I'd made the allegations about the foster parents and I'd recently told her about Patrick Ryan.

'Stay where you are tonight and in the morning I'll come and pick you up and drive you to Marlowe House,' she told me.

By 7.30am we were back in Sidcup.

'Let's go and get a cup of tea in a café before you go in,' she said.

To be honest, I felt like running away and I'm sure Lorna knew that too.

'I'm just going outside for a cigarette,' I told her, with every intention of legging it to the train station as soon as her back was turned. But she wasn't stupid.

'Don't worry, I'll come out with you,' she said.

She talked me into it and at 8am I found myself standing in reception at Marlowe House.

'Just go in and get it over and done with,' she said. 'I'll be down here waiting for you.'

PC Karen Brown was there and she took me up in the lift to the 14th floor. It was a huge open-plan office but we were the only ones in there and it was eerily quiet.

'Let me know if you'd like a cup of tea or a cigarette break,' she told me.

'No thanks, I just want to get on with it,' I snapped, on the defensive as usual.

I was all prepared for her to be horrible and to dislike her, but she was very kind and gentle while still being professional.

It was far from easy, though, and over the next four hours I was forced to remember every little gruesome detail. It was the first time that I'd ever talked to anyone about it and I was amazed how much I remembered. It was almost like I was in a daze, reciting every detail. I knew I had to try and remain emotionless, that was the only way I could get through it. That was the way I'd always dealt with things. If I allowed myself to cry or break down then I knew I wouldn't be able to carry on.

'Debbie, I know you told us in your witness statement how you caught Patrick Ryan abusing Laraine. But how come he started to abuse you?' Karen asked.

'I was nine and the big sister. I wanted to keep her safe,' I said. 'He basically promised me that if I let him abuse me, he wouldn't touch my sister again.'

'Can you recall what Patrick Ryan was wearing when he first attacked you?' Karen asked.

I shuddered at the memory of him still so vivid in my mind.

'He was filthy,' I said. 'He had really dirty fingernails, tatty jeans and a T-shirt that was supposed to be white but it was so grubby and stained.

'If I saw him outside the flat he always had on sunglasses and an old leather jacket and indoors he always wore the same thing too.'

'Did he undress himself when he raped you?' she asked.

'He used to pull down his jeans,' I said. 'Sometimes he still had his dirty white trainers on.'

'Did he ever undress you?'

'Only the bottom half. At that age I didn't have much to interest him up top.'

I was talking about it so matter-of-factly, as if we were discussing the weather. It was so hard trying not to let it get to me, especially when she asked me to describe in detail the things that Patrick Ryan had done to me.

'One of the most upsetting things was the first time he raped me,' I said. 'It hurt so much and I was so shocked, I wet myself so he peed on me. I've never forgotten that. Even today I can't get it out of my head.'

'Debbie, I'm sorry I have to ask you this but at that age how did you know the difference between urine and other bodily fluids? How can you be sure he was urinating on you?'

That's when I told Karen about what my father had done to me.

'Unfortunately, even at nine years old I knew the difference,' I said. 'My father had seen to it that I was no innocent little girl.'

I told her how Ryan hated it if I didn't make a noise and would always force me to keep my eyes open.

'I know it was a long time ago but I remember everything that he ever said to me, the awful names he called me, the terrible threats that he made.

'He threatened to kill us if I told anyone,' I said.

As I talked, Karen wrote it all down in her notebook and then every twenty minutes or so she'd stop and type it up onto her computer.

'Debbie, I know this is so hard for you but you're doing really well,' she told me. 'It's incredible how much you can remember.'

But there was no let-up.

'Now, apart from rape were there any other sexual acts that Patrick Ryan performed?' she asked.

I gulped. This had been the part I was really dreading. For some reason I was OK talking about the rapes, but I found it really difficult to discuss how he'd made me give him oral sex and how he'd done it to me.

My eyes filled with tears but I forced myself not to cry. Karen must have seen I was struggling.

'Take your time, Debbie. I know it's upsetting but it's so important we go over absolutely everything,' she said. 'It's those details that are really going to help the case.'

I knew she was right but I felt so ashamed and dirty; I couldn't even look at her as I described the humiliating things Ryan had done.

'He forced me to give him oral sex,' I said. 'Sometimes he did it to me too. I felt so degraded just having to lie there while he put his tongue or his fingers inside me.'

I couldn't even make eye contact with her. It was horrendous having to tell a stranger such explicit details and afterwards I felt like I was going to be sick.

'Is it OK if we have a break now?' I mumbled, beads of sweat running down my forehead.

'Of course,' she said.

I got up and walked as quickly as I could to the toilet, where I threw up. I was in there for so long, Karen came to find me.

'Debbie, are you all right?' she called.

'Yes, I'm coming now,' I said.

I didn't tell her I'd been sick, though. I didn't want her to think I was weak.

The questions seemed endless but I tried to answer them as best I could. I knew there was one thing Karen couldn't get her head round.

'I need to ask you this, Debbie, but why did you both keep going up there when you knew what Ryan was capable of?'

'Laraine didn't have any friends and Alison was such a sweet girl,' I told her. 'I know it's hard to understand but we were seven and nine; we didn't make rational decisions. I only went up there to protect my sister and after a while the abuse became a way of life. I got so used to it, I just accepted that it was going to happen.'

After four long hours, it was finally over.

'I'll just print out your statement, then I need you to read it through and if you're happy with it to sign it for me,' Karen told me.

I took one look at that statement and I almost fell to pieces. It felt so degrading seeing it there, all written down in black and white, and it really brought home to me what Patrick Ryan had done. My hands were trembling as I signed the bottom.

'Right, that's it, you're all done,' said Karen.

Lorna, bless her, was still waiting for me in reception and she drove me home. There was a bottle of white wine in my handbag and I couldn't wait to get home and open it. But as soon as I got back, I knew the first thing I needed to do was to have a bath.

It was exactly as it had been when I was a girl. Just talking about the abuse had made me feel so dirty that I wanted to try and get myself clean again. I ran a boiling hot bath and soaked in it for nearly an hour. Afterwards I got into the shower and scrubbed myself with a loofah until my skin was red raw. Then I opened the bottle of wine and drank it down, desperately trying to erase the memories of the day from my mind.

'How did it go?' Rob asked when he got home from work.

'It was horrible,' I said.

Only then did I allow myself to cry.

'It brought it all back to me,' I sobbed. 'It's almost like it's happening all over again.'

I hardly slept for the next few days, I was just replaying things over and over in my mind. Mum rang one evening when I'd been drinking as usual. Laraine had told her that she'd made a statement to the police about Patrick Ryan but neither of us had told her about my involvement yet. Mum was really worried about Laraine.

'You know she's back on the booze, Debbie?' she said.

'Yep, she was out of it when I went up there last week,' I told her.

'And all this Patrick Ryan business,' she sighed. 'Surely I would have noticed if my daughter was being abused?'

I was furious.

'No, you wouldn't,' I said. 'You didn't bloody notice when Patrick Ryan raped me or my father for that matter!'

As soon as the words were out of my mouth, I regretted it.

It was totally unforgivable of me to tell her like that but I was drunk and it all came tumbling out. Mum was horrified.

'W-what do you mean?' she stuttered. 'He did it to you, too? And your father?'

'Well, I'm sorry, Mum, but it's all true. That's why I went up to London last week – I was making a statement

201

to the police about what Ryan did to me. How he raped and abused me over a period of three years.

'And you should have known. You're my mum, you should have seen the signs and you didn't notice a bloody thing!'

'Oh, Debbie, I don't know what to…'

But before she could finish, I put the phone down. I didn't want to talk to her.

I was drunk, I was angry and I suppose I needed someone to blame for this whole sorry mess, so I blamed her. She rang my mobile and the home phone but I didn't answer.

'Debbie, please pick up,' she begged. 'I need to talk to you about this. I'm so sorry.'

I could tell she was crying.

Weeks went by but I couldn't bring myself to speak to Mum. She only lived ten minutes away and always came round on a Sunday for a roast dinner but I didn't want to see her.

Rob spoke to her.

'I told her you just need a bit of space,' he said. 'She's shocked and upset too, Deb. This has rocked her to the core. She feels so guilty that she didn't realise what was going on for all those years.'

'Good,' I said.

In the end it was Laraine who got Mum and I talking again. Laraine was drinking more and more, and I was so worried about her. Ironically, I was doing the same thing but because of her past problems, I knew any alcohol could have a very serious and immediate effect on her.

I was so angry with her. She'd set the wheels in motion by going to the police about Patrick Ryan, but at this rate she was doing her best to make sure that she wouldn't be around for any court case, if ever there was one.

'She's going to bloody well kill herself if she's not careful,' I ranted to Rob.

But my anger soon turned to worry. Every day when I rang up, she was drunk. So I swallowed my pride and phoned Mum for the first time in months.

'I'll go up and see her,' said Mum. 'Maybe she'll listen to me?'

She phoned me from her house.

'Debbie, she's really ill,' she said. 'She's all bloated and she can't get out of bed, and when I tried to get her up, she just collapsed.'

'Mum, phone an ambulance.'

'I have,' she said. 'It's on its way.'

I was on tenterhooks, waiting for her to call me back.

Please don't let her die, I thought. I couldn't bear losing my sister as well as my brother.

'I want to go up there and be with her,' I told Rob.

'Just sit tight for now until you know what's happening. There's nothing you can do,' he said.

Mum rang a couple of hours later from Queen Elizabeth Hospital in Woolwich.

'Oh, Debbie, it doesn't look good,' she sobbed.

I could hardly take in what she was telling me. Laraine was in intensive care. Her kidneys had started to fail, she had cirrhosis of the liver and she had internal bleeding in her oesophagus.

'You need to come up now,' said Mum, her voice cracking with emotion. 'The doctors don't think she's going to make it.'

Chapter 15

No More Secrets

I hardly recognised the figure lying in the hospital bed. She was covered in tubes and there were machines bleeping all around her. Any anger I'd felt about her drinking again instantly disappeared the minute I saw her.

I sat on the bed and held her hand.

'Oh, Lal,' I said. 'What have you done to yourself?'

She was drifting in and out of consciousness, so I wasn't sure if she could hear me. The doctors had warned us that she was critically ill and might not pull through but I refused to believe it. I couldn't bear the thought of losing my sister, especially not in the same hospital where my brother had taken his last breath.

'You're going to be all right,' I told her. 'I love you. You'll get through this.'

Her liver was so enlarged she looked seven months pregnant and they were draining litres and litres of fluid out of her. I was shocked at the state that she'd got herself into.

Mum was slumped on a chair in the corner. She looked like she hadn't slept for days and I could see the worry etched on her face. I hadn't seen her for weeks since our argument on the phone and things were still strained between us.

'I can't believe she's done this to herself,' she said. 'I should have realised what was happening to you both. I should have recognised the signs.'

'It's not your fault, Mum,' I said. 'I was just looking for someone to blame.'

'I knew things weren't right but I always put it down to the way your father was and Dad dying. How could I not have realised?'

'There's no point dwelling on the past now,' I told her. 'We just need to focus on getting Laraine better.'

The doctors were doing their best to stabilise her. All we could do was wait. I spent hours pacing up and down the corridors, saying a silent prayer over and over again inside my head.

Please let her pull through. Please let her make it.

We needed nothing short of a miracle and, very slowly, we seemed to get one. As the days passed Laraine started to get stronger. The internal bleeding stopped and her kidneys and liver started to function again. After three days she was moved out of intensive care.

Every few days I went to see her. She was still very poorly and doped up on pain-killing medication but the main thing was she was still alive; it felt like she'd turned a corner. I knew I had to tell her about what Patrick Ryan had done to me. She needed to know now before someone else told her or the police contacted her.

Rob came up to the hospital with me. I was terrified about how she was going to react and I was worried that she'd blame herself for what I'd been through.

'What if it makes her worse?' I said to him. 'She's been through so much, I don't want to tip her over the edge.'

'She needs to know and it's important that she hears it from you,' he said.

He went for a walk while I sat down on the chair next to Laraine's bed. She was still on a drip and very weak.

I took her hand and said, 'There's something I need to tell you. Before you were rushed to hospital I went to see the police to make a statement about Patrick Ryan.'

'I know you did, Deb,' she said. 'You told them about how you'd pulled him off me.'

'No, Lal, this was another statement…'

I paused.

'…about what he did to me.'

Laraine looked puzzled.

'What do you mean, what he did to you?'

'The thing I need to tell you is that he did it to me as well,' I said. 'Patrick Ryan raped me too.'

Laraine looked shocked, completely flabbergasted in fact.

'Oh, Deb,' she said. 'I'm so sorry, I never knew. I never saw him do anything to you.'

'He was a clever bastard, that's why,' I said. 'You see he told me he would stop hurting you if I let him rape me. I was doing it for you. To protect you.'

Laraine started to cry.

'I can't believe you did that for me,' she said. 'But why didn't you tell me? Why did you keep it a secret for all these years?'

I shrugged.

'Because I felt so ashamed and so dirty and disgusting. I never told anyone about it. I tried to forget and even though I couldn't, I didn't want to talk about it.

'When we were little, I don't think I had the words. I was scared and I could see how it had affected you, messing the bed and being so withdrawn and all that.

'That's why I didn't want you to go to the police because I didn't want anyone to know. And I didn't want you to find out because you were drinking so much by then and I didn't want to make it worse.'

'I don't think you could have made things much worse,' she said, giving me a smile through her tears.

I hated seeing her so upset. I could feel my eyes filling up too but I was determined not to cry in front of her. I didn't want to seem weak: I was her big sister, I'd always been forced to be the strong one. I knew I wasn't really inside but that was the act I always put on.

We talked for a while but I could see Laraine was tired.

One of the nurses bustled over to us and said, 'I'm afraid you'll have to go now, visiting time is over.'

I was worried about leaving Laraine in that state but to be honest, I was desperate to get out of there and have a drink.

'Deb, please don't go,' she begged. 'I want you to stay with me for a bit longer.'

'I'm sorry, Lal, I've got to. You heard what the nurse said.'

I gave her a kiss on the cheek as I left.

'It's going to be OK,' I told her, even though I wasn't so sure of that myself. 'I'll be back in a few days.'

It was only when I walked out of the ward and saw Rob waiting for me in the corridor that I broke down. I couldn't keep up the façade any more and I collapsed into his arms.

'You did it, Debbie,' he said. 'You did the right thing.'

I'd been so worried about telling her it actually felt like a huge relief to have that off my chest. For the first time in my life I had nothing to hide and I hoped it helped Laraine to know that she wasn't alone.

Most of all, I realised something had shifted in me. Ever since I'd made my statement, I'd slowly come round to the idea of the case going to court. I'd gone from wanting nothing to do with it to wanting the world to know what Patrick Ryan had done to us. If I blamed anyone for the state Laraine was in, it was him.

I was petrified of him being charged and it going to court but I was even more terrified of no action being taken against him.

I went back to see Laraine a few days later. She'd obviously been thinking about it.

'What did Patrick Ryan do to you?' she asked. 'Was it the same as what he did to me?'

But I was so scared of us jeopardising any court case or putting words into each other's mouths, I couldn't answer.

'I'm sorry but the police said we should try not to talk about specific details that we put in our statements,' I told her. 'We've got to be so careful.'

All I knew was that they'd said our statements were similar. I just wanted Laraine to get better and come home so we could get on with the legal proceedings.

'This is our chance now, Lal,' I said. 'Now everything's out in the open you need to get yourself well so we can make him pay for what he did to us.'

'I don't think I can do it, Deb,' she said. 'I don't think I've got the energy to see it through after everything that's happened.'

I could feel rage building up inside me. She was the one who had said something in the first place and dragged me into this.

'You bloody started all this,' I said.

'And you can bloody well finish it,' she replied.

I prayed that she didn't mean it.

'We shouldn't be arguing about this,' I told her. 'We're in this together.'

With both of us prepared to testify there might be a possibility that there would be a case against Ryan. As the months passed, Laraine grew stronger. She had a major setback when she fell out of bed one day and fractured her pelvis but after four months, the doctors said she was well enough to leave hospital and go home.

'Now you heard what they said,' I told her. 'If you ever drink again it will kill you.'

'I know,' she sighed. 'To be honest, I don't even feel like it.'

She was in a wheelchair and she needed carers to come in and help her at home during the day, while Brendan was out at work. But hopefully, with physiotherapy and rest, she would eventually get her strength back.

It was ironic, really. As Laraine was recovering from nearly dying from alcohol, I was drinking more than ever. I couldn't stop myself.

I was ringing in sick to work and I was like a dog with a bone; I just couldn't let it go. Every day I'd ring the Sapphire Unit and speak to Carol, Jo or Karen, anyone who'd answer, really.

'What's happening?' I'd slur down the phone. 'Is there going to be a trial? Have you heard from the CPS yet?'

'I'm afraid there's no news,' they told me.

I was becoming their worst nightmare. Rob was at the end of his tether, too. I managed to function enough to get the kids their breakfast and get them off to school but after that I'd buy a box of white wine and drink the lot. From the minute I got up to the minute I went to bed, I had a glass of wine in my hand. I was drinking so much I was almost immune to it and I couldn't get drunk any more. God only knows what my poor children were thinking.

'You're going to have to tell the kids what's going on,' said Rob. 'They keep asking me what's wrong with you and why you keep drinking so much. They're not stupid.'

I knew that if it got to a trial they would have to know what was happening anyway, so I sat them all down. Vicky was seventeen by then, Louise was fifteen and Daniel was thirteen. I'd had a drink of course for Dutch courage, but I was still dreading it. How could I explain to a thirteen-year-old boy that his mum had been raped? But I knew that I had to do it.

'I know I've been hard to live with lately,' I told Vicky and Louise. 'But there's been a lot going on and I want you to know why I've been acting like this.

'When Auntie Laraine and I were little we were sexually abused by a neighbour and hopefully it's going to go to court after all this time.'

They were shocked and upset but they didn't cry.

'You can ask me anything you want and I'll be completely honest with you,' I told them.

'What did he do?' Vicky asked.

Calmly I told them about the rape and the things he'd made me do to protect Laraine. I could see they were disgusted.

'I know it's a lot to take in but I also need to tell you about your granddad and what he did to me.'

They were even more horrified because they remembered him.

'I hate him,' said Louise. 'Why did you ever get back in touch with him?'

'That wasn't me,' I said. 'That was your Uncle David's fault.'

In the end I didn't find it hard telling them. What was hard was seeing them so upset, but because I'd had a drink I managed to stay calm.

I was dreading telling Daniel as he was so young but thankfully he didn't ask me about it in any great detail.

'I was sexually abused as a child by a neighbour,' I said. 'Me and Auntie Laraine.'

'What do you mean?' he asked.

'He raped us and made us do these horrible things,' I said.

Bless him, he wasn't embarrassed. It must have been so hard at thirteen to talk about those sort of things with your mum.

'If it goes to court, Mum, I want to come with you,' he told me.

'That's really kind of you, son,' I said, giving him a big hug.

But truth be told if it ever got that far I didn't want my children anywhere near Patrick Ryan.

As the months passed, the police stayed in touch.

'Debbie, the CPS need some more information,' PC Carol Day told me.

They'd already asked for our medical records, our school records, as well as a photograph of the scar above

Laraine's eye where she'd fallen down the stairs. Now they wanted me to draw a layout of the upstairs flat. It felt like it was never going to end.

'All I want to know is if you're going to charge him or not,' I said.

Because if they weren't, I knew I was going to have to take matters into my own hands.

Chapter 16

Off the Rails

I calmly counted up the pills in the palm of my hand: ten diazepam and six sleeping tablets. Before I could think about what I was doing, I took a swig of white wine straight from the bottle and swallowed them all. Then I rested my head on the edge of the bath, sunk down into the deep water and waited for them to take effect.

I knew I couldn't go on like this any more. The stress of waiting to find out if Patrick Ryan was going to be charged was destroying me. I'd been signed off sick from work, so I spent my days drinking and worrying about what was going to happen. Rob and I were constantly arguing and I knew I'd pushed him to the limits.

'I don't think I can go on like this for much longer, Debbie,' he'd told me that night.

He's probably packing his bag now, I thought, as I took another mouthful of wine.

Suddenly my mobile rang and I reached for it on the bathroom floor. It was him.

'I'm sorry, Debbie,' he said. 'I can't carry on the way we are.'

'It's OK,' I said calmly. 'I know I've been a nightmare but don't worry. You ain't going to have to put up with me no more.'

'What do you mean?' he said, panic rising in his voice. 'What have you done? Answer me, Debbie!'

'Bye, Rob,' I said and hung up.

I reached for the bottle of white wine and gulped down the rest in one go. I'd taken too many pills but I didn't care. All I knew was that I didn't want to feel like this any more. Thankfully my body was starting to go numb now, my head was all fuzzy and I was slipping down into the water.

'Open this door, Debbie!' I heard Rob yelling outside, rattling the lock.

But it was as if his voice was coming from somewhere far away. I couldn't move, I couldn't speak. All I could do was sink further and further down until I was fully submerged by the water....

Boom!

There was a massive bang as the bathroom door was kicked off its hinges.

'Debbie, it's the police,' someone shouted. 'We're coming in.'

Suddenly I felt myself being pulled, coughing and spluttering, out of the bath. I stood there, dripping wet and completely naked, in front of three police officers but I was too out of it to care.

Rob was standing by the door, looking worried.

'What the heck are you playing at, Debbie?' he said.

'I don't know,' I mumbled.

I hadn't intended to kill myself but I knew I'd taken enough tablets to do some damage.

'I'm afraid for your own good we're going to have to take you to hospital, Debbie,' said a policewoman.

'Just leave me alone,' I moaned. 'I ain't going anywhere.'

'I'm afraid you either come of your own free will or I'll have to handcuff you,' she said.

She led me to the bedroom and insisted on staying with me while I pulled on some tracksuit bottoms, trainers and a dressing gown. Then she marched me downstairs.

'Right, Debbie, we're going to take you to hospital now,' she said.

'I told you I ain't going nowhere,' I slurred. 'Now piss off!'

'Sorry, Debbie, that's it,' she said, slapping some handcuffs around my wrists.

She led me outside, where a police van and an ambulance were waiting, blue lights flashing.

I bet the neighbours are having a field day, I thought.

I could hear Rob talking to the officers.

'I don't think she meant it,' he said. 'It was just a cry for help.'

They bundled me into the police van and I was taken to Accident and Emergency at Eastbourne Hospital where I worked. I knew a lot of the staff that were on duty but I was too drunk to care.

The on-call psychiatrist was sent to examine me.

'I can't assess her properly because of the amount of alcohol she's drunk,' I heard her say to the nurse. 'I need to come back tomorrow morning when she's sobered up.'

I spent the night on a trolley in A&E so they could observe me. By the next morning, I was terrified they were going to section me. I knew if that happened it would mean an end to any court case.

'I didn't mean to kill myself, I was just drunk,' I told the psychiatrist. 'If I'd really wanted to I would have taken more tablets.'

Thankfully, she believed me.

'We don't believe that you're a suicide risk,' the doctor told me. 'It was just the alcohol talking.'

I was so relieved. A couple of hours later I was discharged and went home. Rob was there. He was upset, but more annoyed than anything.

'You can't keep doing this,' he said. 'It's not fair. How do you think the kids felt, seeing their mum drunk out of her mind, being marched out by the police in handcuffs?'

'I'm so sorry,' I said.

I felt awful but I was on the path to self-destruction and I couldn't stop myself.

The months passed but there was still no update about Ryan and whether or not he would be charged. I felt like my life was on hold until I knew what was happening.

Every week the police or paramedics would be turning up at our house, usually because I'd rung them drunk and made threats or I'd threatened to harm myself. One night I phoned them and said, 'I've got a knife and I'm going to go and find Patrick Ryan.'

I passed out and forgot all about it. A few hours later I'd sobered up, so I took the dog for a walk. I couldn't understand it when I got back later to find the street full of panda cars.

'The police are here again,' said Rob wearily.

'I can see that,' I said. 'What do they want this time?'

I'd forgotten that I'd even called them. I never carried out my threats but they always took me deadly seriously; they had to.

One night when I'd been drinking I rang Victim Support.

'I've had enough,' I told the woman on the phone. 'I can't wait any more to see if there's going to be a trial. I've got a gun here and I'm going to go up to London and find Patrick Ryan, then I'm going to shoot him.'

It was a lovely summer's evening so afterwards I staggered out into the garden where Rob was and knocked back some more wine. Ten minutes later there was a loud rapping at the door. I opened it to find two police officers standing there.

'What do you want?' I said.

'I think you know what we're here for, Debbie,' said the female officer. 'Can we come in?'

'You're going to whether I say yes or no, aren't you?' I said.

I was so aggressive and mouthy but I couldn't help myself.

'Can I come in then?' she said.

'Yes,' I replied. 'If you want a smack in the mouth.'

The next minute she had my hands behind my back and I was being handcuffed. Rob and the kids were all in the garden, wondering what was happening.

I was taken outside while they searched the house. They turned everything upside down looking for the gun. I was just sat there when I happened to glance at the barbecue. The policewoman must have seen me.

'Is there anything in here we should be looking for?' she asked, lifting up the grill.

'Not unless you want a fucking barbecue,' I said.

I was their worst nightmare. I knew I was behaving badly but I didn't care.

Of course I didn't have a gun, so they didn't find anything but Carol phoned the next day.

'This has got to stop, Debbie,' she said. 'You can't go taking the law into your own hands.'

'Well, I've been waiting long enough for you lot to do it so I might have to,' I said.

Ever since I'd given the police my statement, five months ago in January 2012, I'd been having constant nightmares and flashbacks and it wasn't only about Patrick Ryan. I was about to have a counselling session one day when my counsellor Lorna walked through the doors of her office. They were big double doors with a glass panel across the top and as they swung shut I suddenly had a horrible memory about where I'd seen doors like that before. They were just like the ones in mine and David's bedroom at the foster parents' house.

It was like seeing them suddenly triggered something inside me. I felt dizzy and I started to hyperventilate. All of a sudden it was like I was back there at that house. I could see Uncle's piggy eyes peering through the glass, feel Auntie's cold hands touching me under the blankets. Then my father was there, pulling my clothes off.

'Debbie, are you OK?' I heard Lorna ask but I couldn't respond because I knew he was there too.

It was like Patrick Ryan was in the room with me. I could smell his stale, sweaty stench and feel the air being squeezed out of my lungs as he climbed on top of me.

'Get off me!' I yelled. 'Please don't hurt me.'

'Debbie, talk to me,' I heard Lorna say but I was shaking with fear as it felt so real.

In the end Lorna was so worried, she drove me to A&E at Eastbourne General. The psychiatric officer came to examine me and gave me 10mg of diazepam, and very slowly over the next few hours I started to calm down.

'It was like they'd all merged into one and they were all there in the room,' I told her. 'I could feel them on me, abusing me again.'

I'd go to bed and wake up in the middle of the night

screaming. I'd end up punching poor Rob in the face even though he was just lying there minding his own business.

'Get off me!' I'd shout.

'Debbie, it's OK, it's only me,' he'd tell me. 'You're safe.'

I had panic attacks too, along with the flashbacks. One morning I was walking home from the doctor's. One minute I was fine, the next my heart was racing and I was sweating and shaking. It felt like I had pins and needles all over my body and I couldn't breathe. I was halfway up the road, literally yards away from home, but it was as if the nearer I got to my house, the further it moved away.

'Somebody, please help me,' I whispered as I felt my legs give way, but there was no one around.

I knew I was going to keel over so I managed to cling onto a neighbour's wall while I tried to get my breath back, but I couldn't move; I was frozen to the spot. I could see my house but I couldn't get to it.

Eventually I managed to get my mobile out of my bag and phone a cab. The taxi driver must have thought I was crazy as it was literally a one-second journey across the road but I knew I couldn't do it on my own.

It wasn't just the psychological problems either. One of the things I was most ashamed of talking about when I was giving the statement to the police was the fact that Ryan had urinated on me after he'd abused me. It made me feel so dirty and worthless.

When I went to the loo, I'd be sat there and I'd think of him and what he'd done to me, and then I couldn't wee. I was desperate but no matter how hard I tried, nothing came out. It got to a point where it was so bad that I hadn't been able to pass urine at all for three days and I had severe back and stomach ache.

I was too ashamed to go to the doctor's until Mum found me at home doubled over one morning.

'Are you OK?' she asked.

'I haven't wee'd for nearly four days,' I said.

She was horrified and called an ambulance straight away. I was admitted to Eastbourne General again – I think they were sick of the sight of me in there. I lost it when they said they needed to put a catheter in.

'Nobody's touching me down there,' I told Mum.

'It's for your own good, love,' she said.

In the end three nurses had to hold me down while they did it because I was kicking up such a fuss.

'You're very lucky,' the doctor told me afterwards. 'Your bladder was holding three litres of liquid and almost perforated.'

I knew it was extremely dangerous and I could have died. I described my symptoms and they did test after test but they couldn't find any physical reason that would be preventing me from going to the loo. In the end I had to learn how to self-catheterise up to five times a day to stop the same thing happening again.

Just like when we were children, Laraine and I coped

in different ways. Unlike her, I managed to cover up my drinking quite well. I didn't want her to think: 'My God, she's doing the same thing that I did'.

I managed to function to a certain extent. I wasn't falling down drunk and I could always get the kids off to school and make them their tea. But I think she suspected as sometimes I'd ring her up and ask her about the court case.

'Are you OK, Deb?' she'd ask. 'You sound drunk.'

'I've just had a couple of wines,' I'd tell her.

Her way of coping was not to talk about it at all, whereas I was obsessed and that was all I wanted to talk about to anyone. Every day I would phone or text her.

'Do you think he's going to get charged?' I asked her one day. 'Have you heard anything from the police or the CPS?'

'I don't know, Deb. We've done all we can, we'll just have to wait and see.'

'How can you be so matter of fact and calm about it all?' I said, getting annoyed. 'You can't want him to get away with it!'

Laraine sighed.

'Deb, just pack it in,' she said. 'All you ever talk about is him and I don't want to. I'm fed up of hearing about it.'

It made me so angry as she was the one who had started all this.

It was almost like she had closed up after she'd given her statement. It was as if she'd got it off her chest and that was enough, whereas I was the opposite. She wouldn't even discuss it with her own family. It was ages before she'd been able to tell Brendan and the boys what was going on.

'I've told Brendan,' she said. 'It was so hard, Deb, but I did it. He's been really supportive but I don't want him to know any of the details about what happened.'

She'd told Mitchell and Jordan, too.

Eight long months after I'd made my statement against Patrick Ryan, I was at work one day when I saw that I had four missed calls from PC Carol Day.

'Debbie, please can you pick your phone up?' she said in her message. 'It's urgent.'

But whenever I tried to ring her, she was on the other line. I was just coming off my break and walking back to the ward when she rang again.

'Thank God for that,' she said. 'I've got some news for you: Patrick Ryan is going to be charged. The CPS have decided there's enough evidence to prosecute him.'

I literally stopped dead in the corridor.

'What do you mean?' I said, not able to take it in.

'Debbie, there's going to be a court case.'

I was absolutely ecstatic, but in a matter of seconds that quickly turned to dread.

'Oh God, Carol, I don't think I can do this,' I said.

'Yes, you can,' she told me. 'It's thanks to the strength of your evidence and everything that you remembered that this is finally happening.'

My first thought was what Laraine was going to say, but Carol said Jo had already phoned her to tell her.

'When will he have to go to court?' I said.

'We haven't got a definite date yet but anytime from the beginning of September.'

I still couldn't believe it. My hands were shaking as I called Rob and my mum and told them that after all this time it was finally going to court.

Then I rang Laraine.

'We've done it, Lal,' I said. 'They believed us. I'm so pleased that it's going to court.'

But she didn't sound as happy as I'd expected.

'What's wrong?' I asked her. 'Aren't you pleased that it's finally happening after all this time?'

'Course I am,' she said. 'I'm just worried. Deb, we're going to get ripped to pieces in court if there's a trial, you know? There's no evidence – it's just two against one.'

'Well, the police and the CPS must think it's a strong enough case otherwise it wouldn't have gone this far,' I said. 'We should be proud of ourselves.'

'I'm just scared.'

'We can do this together,' I told her.

I was on a high. Without any DNA or forensic evidence, purely on the strength of our statements and the details we could remember, there had been enough to charge him.

The police told us that Ryan would have to appear at Woolwich Crown Court in a couple of weeks. I wasn't surprised when I heard that he'd pleaded not guilty; I was expecting that as he always was a cocky so-and-so.

'It looks like there will definitely be a trial now,' sighed Laraine.

'Good,' I said. 'I'm glad.'

I hadn't wanted him to plead guilty as chances were he would have got a lighter sentence: I wanted him to be found guilty. I wanted the chance to go to court and look him in the eye and tell everyone what he'd done. Finally, after thirty-five years, that was going to happen. It was what I'd waited for and wanted for so long but I was absolutely terrified.

Chapter 17

The Waiting Game

I stood on the pavement and stared at the house in front of me. It looked so familiar yet at the same time so different. The scruffy blue front door that all council houses had in the seventies had been replaced with an original Victorian one that was painted a tasteful shade of bottle green and there was no longer a porch. The tatty, overgrown front garden had been spruced up with new fences, trimmed privets, a tiled path and a wrought-iron gate and the grass neatly mowed.

You see I'd come back to Coleraine Road, or 'the scene of the crime' as the police liked to call it. I hadn't been there for thirty-five years – ever since the day in 1978 when I walked down that path aged twelve, desperate to get away from Patrick Ryan and all that he'd done to us.

Don't ask what had possessed me to come here as I didn't know myself. I'd got up that morning and caught a train to London as I had a day off and was meant to be going to see Laraine. But I'd found myself getting off a couple of stops early at Westcombe Park, and before I could change my mind I was heading in a daze towards

Coleraine Road. It was almost as though I was in a trance as I walked through our old neighbourhood and now there I was, standing on the pavement outside the house which held such horrible memories. Somehow I had needed to come back here and see it for myself. I think part of me also wanted to know if he still lived there.

My hands were shaking as I opened the gate and walked up the front path. I could tell that it had been restored back into one big house now instead of two flats as all the windows had the same louvred wooden blinds on them.

No, it was too big and too grand for a scumbag like him. I bet properties in this street were worth a fortune now.

He doesn't live here any more, I told myself.

But there was one tiny part of me that just wanted to make sure.

I knocked on the door.

What if he was still there? What if he opened it and I was suddenly stood there face-to-face with my rapist after all those years? But I wasn't really thinking straight.

I rapped on it again, louder and more impatient now.

Come on, come to the door. Anyone. Someone.

My heart was thumping out of my chest while I waited and watched for any signs – a twitching curtain, a shadow behind the stained glass panels.

But there was nothing.

It was both a letdown and a relief. I felt a bit stupid

that I'd come all this way to stand on the doorstep of a house where there was nobody in. I wasn't sure what I would have said if somebody had opened it but that didn't matter any more.

I crossed over the road, stood on the pavement and had one last look at my former home. I suddenly realised that I was shaking, even just being there all these years later still had the ability to make me feel like a frightened little girl again. I knew I had to get far away from there. I put my head down and hurried to the end of the street and only then did my breathing start to slow down and return to normal again.

I don't even know how I got to Laraine's and I didn't mention where I had been that morning. I didn't think she'd understand as even I didn't really know what had possessed me to go back.

'You OK, Deb?' she asked. 'You don't seem yourself today.'

'I'm alright,' I said. 'Just tired. This court business is really getting to me.'

When I got home that afternoon, I told Rob what had happened. He was fuming.

'What the hell were you playing at, Debbie?' he said. 'What if Ryan had still lived there and he'd answered the door?'

'I don't know,' I said. 'I really don't know what I was thinking.'

For once I wasn't even drunk. I knew Rob was right

and I was relieved that nobody had been in. If he had still lived there and I'd seen Ryan then it would have probably put the whole court case in jeopardy as I knew I wasn't allowed to approach him.

Even though I knew now there was going to be a trial, I couldn't rest until I had a definite court date. One morning I received a letter from the CPS outlining the charges that Ryan faced. There were four counts of rape, two counts of attempted rape and seven counts of indecent assault. I knew five of the charges related to Laraine and the rest concerned me

Of course Ryan had raped and abused me many more times than that over almost three years, but the police explained that they'd had to condense it down to a handful of charges relating to incidents that we'd specifically remembered. Sample charges, as the judge called them at trial.

Seeing it written down in black and white made it feel even more real. This was really happening. I felt panicked, twitchy, terrified. I was also obsessed with seeing Patrick Ryan. Even though I knew I couldn't approach him before the trial, I was desperate to see what he looked like now.

One afternoon I found myself typing his name into Facebook. Scrolling through all of the photos, I couldn't see a single person that realistically could be him. I'd worked out that he would be a pensioner now, in his early sixties at least. But most of the pictures that came up were of young lads or middle-aged men with kids.

I was finding it so hard. I'd been signed off work again with stress. The CPS still couldn't give us a trial date and it felt like it was dragging on and on. It was mental torture.

Even the police were concerned about my state of mind. Carol and Jo weren't stupid, they knew sometimes I drank too much as I'd phoned them slurring and shouting down the phone. They were also aware of the terrible flashbacks that I'd been suffering in the months since I'd given them my statement.

'Debbie, we're worried about how you're going to cope in court,' said Carol. 'We're concerned that it could tip you over the edge.'

They were trying to prepare me for the fact that even if it went to court, there was no guarantee that Patrick Ryan would be found guilty.

'To be honest, it's highly unlikely that an historic abuse case like this will lead to a conviction and you need to know that,' said Jo.

In my heart I did. After all, it was just going to be mine and Laraine's word against his.

'What's your reaction going to be if he goes free?' said Carol. 'How are you going to cope with that?'

'Honestly?' I said. 'I don't know.'

I was worried when they said that both Laraine and I needed to be assessed by a psychiatrist, who would judge whether we were physically and mentally fit to go to court

'We have to be,' I said to Rob. 'Otherwise this case will fall apart.'

If I were deemed unfit then without my evidence, I was convinced there would be no court case. Even if they ruled Laraine was OK, I knew that her evidence on its own wasn't going to be enough.

Rob came with me up to Marlowe House, where the psychiatrist had arranged to interview me. I was so nervous but she seemed like a nice woman and she instantly put me at ease. She was in her thirties with blonde hair and a friendly smile.

'I'm not here to try and catch you out,' she said. 'The police have got your best interests at heart. I'm here to assess you and discern what impact a court case is going to have on you.'

She said she'd already requested statements from my GP and Lorna, my counsellor.

'Mrs Grafham, how do you think you would cope if Mr Ryan wasn't found guilty?' she asked.

'I would prefer it if he was, of course,' I said. 'But as long as I get a chance to go to court, then I know that I've done everything I can to try and get a conviction.'

'How do you feel about seeing him again?' she continued.

'Don't bother me,' I shrugged. 'I know he can't get to me any more.

'Like I told you, I just want to have my day in court. I know I've had issues in the past where I've threatened to self-harm but that was brought on by the alcohol and I've really cut down now.'

I was in there for nearly two hours.

'Thank you for coming, Mrs Grafham,' she said. 'I'll put together a report which I'll pass onto the police and I'm sure they will be in touch.'

When I got home I texted Jo and Carol.

Did she say I was fine to go to court because I know I am?

They told me it could take weeks for the report to come through but I still texted them every day, asking if they'd got any news.

Exactly a fortnight later I received a big envelope from the police with a copy of the psychiatrist's report inside.

My hands were shaking as I read it.

In my professional opinion I feel that Mrs Grafham would be able to withstand the intense questioning that she would be subjected to during the trial process without it having a detrimental effect on her health.

I believe her determination is a key factor of her ability to cope with this. The fact that she now feels believed has led to her using the support that has been offered to her rather than internalising her distress as she has done in the past. It is not my clinical opinion that Mrs Grafham is at risk of suicide or self-harm.

It was such a relief.

'They've ruled I'm fit to go to court,' I told Rob.

But a few days later there was a huge blow. The police got in touch to say that although the psychiatrist had said that I was fine, there was a problem with Laraine. The same psychiatrist had been to interview her at home and had expressed concerns when she'd seen Laraine was still very weak and bedbound after her time in hospital.

'We think it's likely she's going to come back and say your sister's not fit to go to court,' Carol told me.

I was devastated and I felt angry with Laraine even though I knew it wasn't her fault.

'I'm sorry, Deb,' she said. 'But I just told her the truth. I don't think I would physically be able to get to court, even if I'd wanted to.

'You know I haven't even got out of bed or left the house since I came home from hospital.'

'You could get a wheelchair,' I said.

'I just don't think I could cope with all those questions and seeing him sitting there right next to me,' she said.

I know I shouldn't have been, but I was furious with her. I feel bad about it now but I wasn't nice to her at the time.

'You were the one that started this and I always said I never wanted to get involved or for it to go to court,' I told her. 'And now you're not well enough, you're off the bloody hook and you've landed me right in it!'

'I'm sorry, Deb,' she said.

I felt responsible. It was going to be down to me to stand up in court, in front of a jury and tell everyone what he'd done. It should have been both of us there, side by side.

'So much for being in this together,' I said to Rob. 'I can't do it on my own. I don't think I can go.'

But luckily all hope was not lost. The police got in touch again.

'As we thought, the psychiatrist has ruled that Laraine is not medically fit to attend court,' said Carol.

My heart sank.

'But she has said that she thinks that she's mentally fit to give evidence during the trial via video link from home.'

I was still annoyed that Laraine was off the hook from attending court but it was the best result that I could have hoped for. I think Laraine was just relieved. I still felt she'd got the easy way out as I was the one who was going to have to face Patrick Ryan in the flesh but at least it meant the trial was going to go ahead.

At long last a trial date was set for 23 April 2013. In November, five months before the case was due to start, the police invited me up to Woolwich Crown Court to have a look around.

'I know you've never set foot inside a courtroom before, Debbie, so I thought it might help you feel more comfortable,' Carol explained.

I knew exactly what the court looked like from the outside because I'd googled it so many times. Of a night

I'd sit there in front of my computer staring at the photo of this big grey modern building with circular pillars, imagining the day that I would step foot in there to see Patrick Ryan for the first time.

Carol picked us up from Plumstead station and drove us there. The court was tucked away on an industrial estate and I noticed that it was next to Belmarsh Prison.

I bet that's where Ryan will go if he's found guilty, I thought to myself.

I could only hope.

At the front was a modern glass entrance which was a bit like being in an airport. You had to walk through metal detectors to get in and security guards searched your bags.

'I'm going to show you around two courts,' explained Carol, 'although we won't know until the day of the trial which one it's going to be in. It depends what other cases are going to be heard that day.'

As we followed her down the winding corridors, I felt sick. The next time I was going to be there it would be to face him and even the thought of it was terrifying. We went into courtroom four first and I was shocked by how small it was.

It was all on one level and Carol showed me the witness box where I would be giving evidence and explained how the jury would be sat opposite me and the judge would be to my left at the front of the court.

'That's the dock where Ryan will be,' she said.

'He'll be behind a glass screen with a security guard next to him.'

It was slightly behind the witness box and to the right, but that court seemed so small and claustrophobic it felt like he would practically be sat next to me.

'That's way too close for comfort,' I said.

I really hoped that it would be in the bigger court. That one seemed huge and had two levels with rows of seats for the press and a big public gallery on the second level. The dock felt like it was over the other side of the room and was much further away from the witness box.

Carol talked me through the proceedings. The first time I would be allowed in court was the day that I was due to give evidence.

'You'll be the last one into court on the day,' she explained. 'So everyone else will already be seated when you come in, including Ryan in the dock.'

Even the thought of it made my stomach lurch with nerves.

'What do you think they'll ask me?' I said.

'They'll ask you about your statement and they will want to know details about the abuse and Ryan.

'There's no point lying to you, Debbie. It's going to be hard and at times it might feel as if you're the one on trial and not Ryan.

'Remember, his barrister is there to defend him, so he's not going to give you an easy time. But you're telling the truth and I know you can do it.'

It was terrifying and there was so much to remember.

'When you get asked a question by the barrister, or perhaps the judge, obviously look at them when they're talking but try and direct your answer to the jury,' said Carol.

'Also, try not to look at Ryan as that could be classed as intimidation. There will be screens there on the day if you want them so he can't see you when you give your evidence.'

'No way,' I told her. 'I've always said from the start that if it ever got to court then I didn't want to hide behind a screen.'

I was adamant.

'I've got nothing to hide,' I said. 'I want that man to see me and to hear exactly what he did to me.'

When Patrick Ryan was raping me he'd always made me keep my eyes open. Whatever disgusting thing he was subjecting me to, he'd always forced me to look at him. Well, the tables had well and truly turned now and I was determined that this time he would be forced to look at me while I told the world what he'd done.

'I'm 100 per cent sure I don't want a screen up,' I insisted.

As I left court that day, I felt a mixture of nerves and anticipation. The next time I would set foot in that place I would be coming face-to-face with Patrick Ryan.

Chapter 18
D-Day

I got out of the car and smoothed down my new smart black trousers and my crisp white blouse.

'Good luck,' called Rob's dad from the driver's seat.

'Thanks, Dad,' said Rob. 'We'll give you a ring when it's finished for the day.'

It was Tuesday, 23 April 2013. The first day of the court case, or 'D-Day' as I referred to it. I'd been waiting so long for this moment but now I was dreading it. I'd been awake for most of the night, tossing and turning, and I was absolutely shattered.

My phone beeped with a message from Carol.

Text me when you're here and I'll come down and get you.

I texted back.

Two minutes away.

As we walked towards the court, I gripped Rob's hand. A couple of minutes later I saw Carol waiting for us at the entrance.

'How are you doing, Debbie?' she asked.

I just shrugged, worried that if I spoke I'd break down again.

'It's going to be OK,' she said. 'There's nothing to be frightened about. Jo and I will talk you through it all.'

She was lovely and I knew she was doing her best to reassure me, but no one really knew how I felt. No one except Laraine, that is.

'The case is going to be in court four today,' said Carol.

My heart sank. I remembered from when we'd had our tour that that was the small one. I was literally going to be a few feet away from Patrick Ryan when I gave my evidence.

'Don't worry,' said Rob, squeezing my hand. 'It will be fine. I'll be there.'

He went off to sit in the public gallery while Carol explained the timings of things.

'Laraine's due to give evidence this morning via video link, then it will be your turn this afternoon,' she said. 'Now Ryan's got quite a few family members with him, so it's probably best if you stay in the witness room until you're called and don't go outside on your own.'

I couldn't believe anyone was standing by him after what he'd been accused of.

She led me to a tiny room where Lorna, my counsellor, was waiting. She'd agreed to come with me for moral support and I was so pleased to see her. I never had to put on a brave face with her.

'I don't think I can do this, Lorna,' I said.

'You just need to go in there and tell the truth and that's all that matters,' she told me. 'We're all here for you.'

There was a small glass panel in the door and I could see the outline of people going past into court four. I was terrified at the thought that one of them was Patrick Ryan.

There was a TV in the witness room with DVDs but I had no interest in watching them; there was also a bookcase filled with books and a little kitchen off the back.

'Do you want a cup of tea, Debbie?' asked Lorna.

'No, thanks,' I said. 'I feel a bit sick.'

I hadn't managed to eat or drink anything that morning, my stomach was so churned up.

I couldn't sit still, so I paced up and down.

We were the only ones in there at first but as time went on, people from different cases were coming in and out. I kept opening the door and going out and having a look around outside to see if I could see anyone going into the courtroom.

'Debbie, come back in and sit down. You know what the police told you,' said Lorna.

I think she was worried that I was going to leg it. Part of me did feel like running away from there but I knew that after everything we'd been through, I had to do this.

I looked at the clock. Just after 10am.

'Laraine should have started giving her evidence now,' I said. 'I hope she's doing OK.'

More than anything I wanted to be in that courtroom to see how she was getting on. I was so worried about how she was going to cope with being cross-examined and

I wanted to be there for her. It was so frustrating being stuck in this little room while my poor sister was being put through hell and there was nothing I could do to help.

Carol and Jo had explained that one of them would be in the house when Laraine was giving her evidence, but they weren't allowed to be in the bedroom with her in case they gave her prompts. Laraine didn't want Brendan to be there so he'd gone to work.

To be honest, I was mortified that the jury would have to see her like that, lying there in her nightie, unable to get out of bed and reliant on carers. In my mind Ryan had done that to her and she was so vulnerable.

'I really feel for her,' I told Lorna. 'At first I thought she had the easy option with the video link. But I don't know what's worse – having to be here in court or having to give evidence from your own home, lying in bed all on your own.'

I really hoped she could do it.

Suddenly my mobile phoned beeped with a text from her.

Oh, Deb, the video link's not bloody working.

'I'm going to go outside and ring her,' I said to Lorna. 'I need to know what's going on.'

I knew it was safe because everyone else was in court. When I spoke to Laraine, she sounded so frightened.

'Hopefully the link will be sorted soon and you can get on with it,' I said.

'Deb, I'm scared,' she told me.

'It's going to be all right,' I said. 'I just wish I could be with you, holding your hand. You can do this.'

I was trying to be strong for her and sound positive while deep down I was as frightened as she was that he might be going to get away with this. I just prayed that giving evidence by video link would have the same impact on the jury as if she was standing there in court.

I spent the next couple of hours pacing up and down, driving Lorna demented. All this waiting was torture. Finally, just before 12.45pm, the door to the witness room swung open and Rob came in.

'What happened?' I said. 'Did they get the link working? How did Laraine do? Did you see him? What did he look like?'

'Calm down, Debbie,' he said.

He explained that they couldn't get the video link working for over an hour.

'It took ages,' he said. 'We were all just sitting there, but thankfully they managed it in the end.'

'How was Laraine?' I asked. 'Did she cope OK?'

'She did really well,' he told me. 'She got a bit jumbled with a couple of the dates and she got really upset at one point but I think it went OK.'

It was such a relief.

Poor Lal. My heart ached for her, having to go over those horrible memories, for everyone having to hear what she went through.

'The judge cleared the courtroom at one point so she

could have a break and a cigarette and she seemed a bit more composed after that,' he added.

I was so proud of her.

'What's the jury like?' I asked Rob.

'There's eight women and four men,' he said. 'They're all different ages. There's a young lad and then one or two blokes my age and the foreman is an older man in his fifties.'

I was relieved to hear that there were more women than men. Hopefully they would understand how hard it was going to be for me to talk about all these intimate things.

'What about him?' I said. 'What does he look like?'

'He's a nasty piece of work, just like you said,' he told me.

I was desperate to see him before I gave evidence.

Carol came in to update us.

'It went really well,' she told me. 'Laraine answered all the questions and she was really strong. Now you've got about forty minutes, so why don't you go and get some lunch?'

I didn't feel like eating anything but I wanted to get out of that windowless, airless room.

'Where can we go?' I said to Rob.

'Well, I don't think we should go to the canteen because Ryan and his lot will probably be there,' he said. 'Let's go for a walk.'

There was a little Tesco's where Rob's dad had

dropped us off that morning so me, Rob and Lorna walked up there to get a sandwich, although I couldn't manage more than a couple of mouthfuls.

All the time I was constantly looking around for Ryan. I was terrified but at the same time desperate to see him so I knew what he looked like before I gave my evidence. I was worried about what my reaction might be and wanted to get it over and done with before I set foot in that courtroom.

'I'm gagging for a cigarette,' I said, and as we walked back towards the court I noticed there was a little walled area with some benches and a few trees where people were lighting up.

'I think I'll just go and sit over there and have a smoke,' I said.

But Rob suddenly grabbed my arm and pulled me back.

'No, you're not,' he said.

'What do you mean, I'm not? Where else can I have a ciggy?'

'Debbie, don't go over there,' he said. 'Come with me, keep walking and don't look round.'

I could hear the panic in his voice and that's when I knew Ryan was there. The minute he said it I turned round to look and I recognised him straight away.

He was sat there on one of the benches smoking, looking like he didn't have a care in the world. Wendy was with him and a younger woman that I didn't recognise.

The first thing that struck me was the massive gauze dressing stuck over his left eye.

'What the hell is that bandage on his face?' I said to Rob. 'Is that to cover up his dodgy eye?'

'They said in court that he'd injured his eye in a welding accident when he was sixteen and it had been giving him trouble all his life, so he'd recently had an operation to remove it,' he told me.

'Going for the sympathy vote, no doubt,' I said.

I knew Ryan hadn't seen me so I stared at him, willing him to turn round.

For months I'd been planning this moment in my head. All the things I wanted to say, like why had he picked on us? But then I saw him and I was taken aback. He looked like an old man. A pathetic old man, come to that. His hair was grey, his shoulders were stooped and he was hunched over. I wasn't frightened of him any more, in fact I almost laughed. He looked the smartest that I'd ever seen him in a navy blue jumper with a white shirt underneath but his horrible face was still the same.

I could see Rob was nervous and he quickly ushered me away.

'Come on, Debbie, let's get inside,' he said.

Just then I got a text from Carol.

Ryan is outside, Debbie, so just be careful and come straight back in to the witness room.

It made me angry.

'I'm not the one on bloody trial but I feel like the

prisoner here and not him,' I said. 'If I want to go outside and smoke then I should be allowed.'

'The police are only thinking of your own safety, Debbie,' Rob told me. 'There's quite a group of them and I don't want any trouble. That's not going to help the case.'

I knew he was right but I was glad that I had seen Ryan. I hadn't gone to pieces and it had made me feel a bit stronger. Maybe I could do this?

The court was due back, so Rob went to take his seat in the public gallery and I went back to the witness room with Lorna.

'How are you holding up, Debbie?' asked Carol.

'OK,' I said, but when my voice came out it was barely a whisper.

I was absolutely terrified

'You can do this,' said Lorna. 'Just go in there and tell the truth.'

Jo came down

'It's time,' she said. 'We'll take you up.'

I was in a daze. This felt like it wasn't really happening to me and I was having some strange out-of-body experience. My legs were so shaky as I followed Carol and Jo down the corridor I thought I might fall over. We went past the canteen and down a long corridor, through some double doors until I saw the sign for court four.

Oh God, this was really happening. Any minute now I was going to have to face him. My heart was thumping so hard, I could practically hear the blood pumping through my body. My head was spinning and I was so tired, I felt delirious.

We stopped right outside the court door. Just as we were about to go in, it swung open and a man in a black cloak and wig came out. He looked exactly like someone from one of those courtroom dramas that you see on the TV.

'This is the prosecution barrister, Mr Williams,' Jo explained.

'I'm awfully sorry, Mrs Grafham,' he said. 'But I'm afraid one of the jurors has been taken ill at lunchtime with toothache.

'We can't continue without a full jury, so I'm afraid it looks like we're going to have to adjourn for the day.

'Do you mind coming back tomorrow?'

It was a huge blow. I was annoyed about the delay but overwhelmed with relief at the same time.

'Excuse me,' I said.

I ran down the corridor and rushed into the nearest toilet, where I was violently sick. I think my body had gone into shock.

Carol came to find me.

'Are you OK, Debbie?' she asked.

'It's just nerves,' I said. 'I was all psyched up to go in.'

'I know you were,' she said. 'But try and get some sleep tonight and then you can get it over and done with tomorrow.'

It was such a let-down.

Rob came out to find me.

'I can't believe it's been postponed,' he said.

'Let's get you both back to the witness room,' said Carol. 'I think it's safer for you to wait there until we know Ryan and his family have gone.'

We waited in there another hour before we walked to Tesco's, where we'd arranged for Rob's dad to pick us up. As soon as we got back, I phoned Laraine. Carol had already called her to tell her that I wasn't giving evidence until tomorrow.

'How was it?' I said. 'I've been thinking about you all day.'

'Oh, it was awful, Deb,' she told me. 'The things they asked me, it was horrible.'

'I know,' I said. 'Rob told me. It must have been really hard.'

She said that she'd been questioned for an hour and a half.

'I got really upset when they kept asking me why did we keep going up there, but all I could say was that I didn't know. I can't answer that, even to this day.

'I kept saying I just went up there to play with Alison. I was only seven, I didn't know what I was thinking but his barrister gave me a really hard time about it.

'I'm just glad it's over.'

'You did so well,' I told her. 'I'm so proud of you, Lal. It's my turn tomorrow.'

'Did you see him, Deb?' she asked. 'What did he look like?'

'Yeah, I saw him outside smoking at lunchtime,' I said. 'He looked just the same but older and he hasn't got a ponytail any more. He's horrible, Lal, he just looks like a pathetic old man.'

'Oh well,' she sighed. 'We'll just do the best we can, Debbie, and see what happens.'

But that wasn't good enough for me. I wouldn't be satisfied with anything other than a guilty verdict.

That night, me, Rob and his dad went out to dinner at the local pub. I hardly ate anything and I didn't even have a drink. That was the hardest thing for me. There was nothing I felt like more than downing a bottle of white wine but I knew I had to keep a clear head. I couldn't go to court and give evidence with a hangover.

'If you come into court under the influence, you won't be able to give evidence and it's game over,' Carol had already warned me.

I didn't want to do anything that would risk it.

Later on the kids phoned to see how it had gone but I couldn't bring myself to speak to them. I knew if I heard their voices, I would break down and I didn't want them to know I was upset.

'Will you tell them what happened?' I said to Rob.

In hindsight maybe it was a good thing I wasn't called to give evidence that day as I was a wreck. It had given me a dry run in a way. I'd seen the court, I'd seen Ryan. Now I felt better prepared.

I knew I desperately needed to get some sleep, so I took some diazepam, just enough to knock me out but not enough so that I'd feel groggy in the morning. It did the trick and I managed to get three or four hours.

I woke up the next morning and then it hit me.

'Today's the day,' I said to Rob. 'I honestly don't think I can do it.'

'Deb, you're going to be fine,' he told me. 'Just stand up in that court and tell the truth and that will be enough.'

I prayed he was right.

The reason I had to get through this was because of Ryan. All the years of suffering that I'd been through were because of him.

'I haven't come this far to see him get off,' I said.

I was so determined that I was going to make him pay for what he'd done to Laraine and me.

The police had advised us to get there early to try and avoid Ryan and his family but as we walked up to the court entrance, they were all out front again, having a smoke.

'Put your head down and just keep walking,' said Rob, putting a protective arm around me.

But I had nothing to be ashamed of. I looked straight at Ryan and this time he saw me. For a split second we locked eyes and he just glared at me. He still had that gauze dressing over his dodgy eye.

He was only sixty-four but he looked like an old man. I wasn't frightened or scared but I still felt humiliated. It made me angry that he still had the power to make me feel so ashamed all these years later.

If Rob and Lorna hadn't been with me, steering me away, then I knew I would have gone over to him and given him a mouthful. Just seeing him sat there was enough to make me want to go over and kill him with my bare hands. I was so determined to make him face justice. I wanted to make him pay for his crimes and I knew the only way that I could do that was through the court.

'Come on, Deb,' said Rob, ushering me inside.

Lorna and I went straight to the witness room while Rob took his place in the public gallery.

'Good news, the case has been moved to court one today,' Carol told me.

It was such a relief that it was going to be in the bigger court as it meant Ryan would be much further away from me.

At 10am on the dot, Jo came down to the witness room.

'Debbie, they're ready for you now,' she said.

I was so nervous, I couldn't even reply.

'Don't worry,' she said. 'Just tell the truth.'

I'd been waiting for this moment for so long that it didn't seem real. Here we were again. Down another corridor, through some double doors and then we were suddenly standing outside courtroom one.

'Debbie, I just want to doublecheck one last time, that you're sure you don't want a screen up when you're giving evidence so that Ryan can't see you?' asked Carol. 'There's one in the courtroom. It'll only take two minutes to put it up.'

'I'm sure,' I said. 'I don't want no screen – I want him to see me. I've got nothing to hide.'

Jo pushed open the door and I took a deep breath and went in. It felt like everyone's eyes were on me as I walked across the courtroom towards the witness box. The first person I saw was Patrick Ryan, sat on the right in the dock behind a glass screen. He was slouched on a chair with his leg up and his elbow resting on his knee, a security guard flanking him on one side. He didn't look nervous and he didn't show any reaction when I walked in, but as I walked across the court to the witness box, I could feel him watching me.

The jury was a sea of faces straight ahead of me. There were a couple of young people and some women who looked to be around my age. I knew the man at the far left was the foreman and he was in his fifties.

As I stepped into the witness box, I was shaking like a leaf. I felt totally out of my depth. I could see both barristers sat there at the front and I was terrified about what they were going to ask me.

The court usher, an older lady in a black robe, held up a bible and I had to swear on it. There was a microphone and it felt strange hearing my voice, quivering with nerves, echoing around that huge courtroom.

After I'd taken the oath, Judge Tomlinson turned to me and said, 'Mrs Grafham, please take a seat.'

'No, thanks,' I said. 'I'd prefer to stand.'

I'd been obsessed with this day for so long but now I was actually here it didn't seem real.

'I must say it's very commendable of your witness not to have any screens up,' I heard Ryan's barrister say to Mr Williams, the prosecution barrister.

But I didn't feel commendable. I felt terrified out of my wits because I knew whatever happened next wasn't going to be nice.

Chapter 19

Justice

First up was the prosecution barrister Mr Williams, who I'd met the day before. I was still nervous but at least I knew he was on my side.

'Mrs Grafham, I am going to ask you some questions. May I call you Debbie as I do that?'

'Yeah, that's fine,' I said.

'Thank you,' he replied. 'When I have finished asking you some questions the gentleman who sits to my right, Mr Collings, will ask you some questions.'

'OK,' I said.

'Can you give your answers, when you do answer the questions, not to either of us but rather to the ladies and gentlemen in the jury box over there?

'And keep your voice up if you would and try and reach the back row, but that microphone might assist.'

I nodded. The hard part was about to begin.

At first it was just basic information that he was asking. How old were we when we lived at Coleraine Road? Who lived in our flat? How long did we live there? How did we know Patrick Ryan?

I had to keep reminding myself whom to look at and when and I was so worried that I was going to mess it up.

'Are you able to say anything about an incident that concerned Laraine when she was in the upstairs flat that you became aware of?' Mr Williams asked.

Carol had told me he wasn't allowed to be seen to be putting words into my mouth with his questions but I knew straight away what incident he was referring to.

'Yes, I had been out,' I said. 'I had been to the park and I had come back and I heard Laraine screaming and crying. The front door was open.'

'Where were the screams and the crying sounds coming from?'

'It was from the upstairs flat,' I explained. 'So I went up there.'

'And what did you see when you went up the stairs?'

'Patrick Ryan on top of my sister on the landing.'

'What did you do when you saw Patrick Ryan on top of your sister on the landing?'

'I tried to get him off,' I said. 'I jumped on his back and I tried to pull him by his ponytail. He let go of my sister. Whether he fell or she fell I don't know but she went down the stairs.'

'How was she once she got to the bottom of the stairs?' he asked.

'She was upset. She was crying and she had a cut on her face. I took her in and bathed her face and her glasses were broke.'

We quickly moved onto the stuff I was dreading.

'Was there ever any incident in which you were involved with Patrick Ryan?' asked Mr Williams.

'Yes, on several occasions,' I replied.

'I am going to ask you to tell us about each of those in some detail,' he said.

I took a deep breath. The questions kept coming – what was I wearing? What exactly did he do? Where were we in the house? What had happened afterwards? He wanted to know everything.

'I am going to move on to the first time that you remember that Mr Ryan put his penis into your vagina. Firstly, where did that take place?' he asked.

'I saw him again with Laraine and I begged him and begged him to stop it, to stop touching her,' I told him. 'The conditions were if I let him do it to me then he would stop touching my sister.'

'What did he then go on to do?'

'He went on to rape me fully.'

'How did that rape come about?'

'Laraine was up there again with Alison and more often than not I would go up with her because I knew what was going to be happening to her. He was going to do it to Laraine again if I didn't let him do it to me.

'He got hold of me before I got to the front room,' I said.

'And what did he do when he got hold of you?'

'He took my bottoms off and forced my legs apart. Then he forced his penis into my vagina so hard.'

'How did you feel when he forced his penis into your vagina?'

My hands were sweating now and I was worried I was going to pass out. I gripped onto the sides of the witness box to stop myself from keeling over. I gulped down some water. God only knows how many glasses I'd already got through.

'Jesus, it fucking hurt!' I said. 'It burnt and made me wee. It made me wee, it hurt so much.'

That was the only time I lost it and swore. Thankfully no one pulled me up on it or told me off. I just felt so dirty and embarrassed.

'What was Patrick Ryan's reaction when you wee'd?'

'He called me a dirty little c**t,' I said, still feeling ashamed at the memory. 'That's what he called me.'

'How long did he have sex with you?'

'It felt like forever but probably minutes. I was just trying to fight and...'

'And how did it come to a conclusion?'

'He ejaculated inside me.'

'After he had raped you what was the state of your vagina?'

'It was burning. It was bleeding.'

'What did he do once he had finished raping you?

'He pissed on me.'

I could feel the jury's eyes on me. It was so hard describing these horrific, intimate things that happened to me in front of a room full of strangers as well as the man who had done it.

I could see some of the jury members were as distressed as I was. I kept catching the eye of one woman who looked like she was in her early forties like me. I could see her eyes filling up with tears as I answered. I felt for them. It must have been horrible having to sit there and hear that and also for poor Rob, sat there in the public gallery, listening to how I was abused and humiliated.

I tried to answer everything clearly and confidently but it was so hard. I knew it was going OK because Carol was sitting at the front of the court with Jo and every so often I'd catch her eye and she'd give me a thumbs up. But I was so scared about what was to come.

'What other incidents were there that directly involved you?' Mr Williams asked.

This was the part that I was really dreading.

'He would also put his penis in my mouth and then he would on other occasions pull my shorts or my trousers down and he would put his tongue inside my vagina,' I said, shuddering at the memory.

'Where was it that that would happen?'

'On the landing, always mainly on the landing.'

'And how long did each episode of that behaviour go on for?'

'It's hard to put a timing on it. It felt like forever.'

'And, again, approximately how many times did that behaviour happen that he put his tongue inside your vagina?'

'Oh God, it was lots,' I said. 'I didn't count but lots.'

As I was forced to describe in detail to the court how Ryan had pushed his penis into my mouth and moved my head backwards and forwards on it, vomit fizzed in my throat.

Oh God, please don't let me be sick in the witness box, I thought.

I could feel the colour drain from my face. Mr Williams must have noticed it too because he said, 'Would you like to take a break, Debbie?'

There was nothing I would have liked more. I was desperate to get out of that courtroom and have a cigarette, but I think if I'd left at that point I wouldn't have gone back. I also remembered what Carol had told me before the trial started: 'They'll probably ask you if you want to break but if you can manage it it's best to say no because it interrupts the flow of questioning,' she'd said.

'No, thank you,' I told him.

'Are you happy to carry on?'

'Yes,' I nodded.

I knew the sooner I got this over and done with, the sooner I could go.

The questions carried on.

'Why didn't you tell your mother about what he was doing to Laraine and what he had been doing to you?'

'My mum was never really around. She wasn't well and part of me was ashamed and part of me, I suppose, was used to it by the time he started doing it.'

'I did threaten to tell my mum and he told me his brother was in the police force and I would never be believed and that he would kill us and he would kill my mum.'

Thankfully, I couldn't see Ryan as I gave evidence. But if I turned around slightly to the right and looked over my shoulder then I could catch a glimpse of him. I did have the odd sneaky glance at the dock but he was always looking at the floor.

'Thank you, Debbie,' Mr Williams said to me finally. 'I have no more questions, Your Honour.'

At least that part was over with, but now it was Ryan's barrister's turn to question me and I knew that what had just gone was a walk in the park compared to what was to come.

Don't let him get to you, I told myself.

I took a deep breath and prepared for battle. I was right to have been worried: Mr Collings pulled no punches.

'You may know this, you may not,' he told me. 'But Mr Ryan does not accept that he perpetrated any sexual abuse against either you or your sister back in the early seventies. That is our starting point in relation to the defence case. You understand that?'

'I understand,' I said.

He firstly questioned why, when I went to the police about the abuse from the foster parents, hadn't I mentioned then that I had also been abused by Ryan?

'I didn't mention it because Laraine hadn't mentioned it then and neither of us spoke about it,' I told him. 'We never spoke to each other about the abuse at all.'

He seemed to be implying that I was distressed that I hadn't been able to get justice for the foster parents, so therefore I had picked on Ryan.

'Isn't it right, Debbie, that what you needed and what you wanted really was a name so that you could get justice?' said Mr Collings. 'Would that be fair to say?'

'In relation to the foster parents, yes, but Mr Ryan was nothing to do with that case,' I said.

'But isn't that one of the reasons that you have come forward now at this late stage in relation to Mr Ryan, because it is your perception of getting justice for what happened to you?'

'No,' I told him. 'Not at all.'

'Because, of course, Mr Ryan is saying that you are lying about what happened and making it up.'

'I'm not lying,' I said. 'Honestly, I'm not lying at all.'

I tried not to let him get to me but I felt so angry I was shaking.

'Why, if this was going on so extensively, as you say, and your younger sister was being abused as well, did you not tell your mother?'

'She was ill all the time and I was scared that we would be taken away from her and put in a foster home again. She had enough to worry about.'

'Can you remember were Social Services still involved

with the family when you were in Coleraine Road?' he asked. 'Do you remember social workers coming round at all?'

'I really honestly can't remember,' I said.

'Were there teachers at school, anybody that you could have told about this?'

'I didn't trust anybody,' I said. 'I didn't trust anybody after that, no.'

'Debbie, you are saying that this abuse went on and you allowed your sister to go upstairs, yes? Did you never try to stop Laraine from going upstairs?'

'Of course I did,' I told him. 'She kept going up there because Alison wanted her to go so that's when I went with her.'

'On how many occasions did that happen?'

'Again, it was quite a few occasions. I can't put a number on it.'

'And you, yourself, of course, kept going back, yes?'

'Yeah,' I said. 'Yes, I did.'

I felt like telling him where to go but I was determined not to lose my cool or show myself up in front of the jury.

'You weren't there and I was,' I said. 'Nothing you say is going to make me retract anything that I said in my statement because it's all true.'

I could feel the anger rising up inside me. It had always been my biggest fear that no one would believe us and now this man was trying to make out that I was a liar and had made it all up. I know he was only doing his job but there was no let up.

'It didn't happen, did it, that you played, as you say, with Alison?'

'It did happen,' I said. 'I was there, I know. I know what I done, I know what happened.'

'And this free range, as it were, of you children roaming around this house, playing with Alison whenever you wanted to. It simply didn't happen, did it?' said Mr Collings.

'It did happen. I know what happened and I stand by it.'

'And the reason, can I suggest to you, Debbie, in relation to your disclosure, really, as to what happened to you is this, that it simply isn't true, is it?'

'It is true,' I said.

'And for whatever reason, you have decided to support your sister in relation to the disclosure that she has given.'

'No, that's not the case at all.'

'Because you, in fact, have decided, have you not, that the justice that you seek to get is going to be in relation to Mr Ryan?'

'No, that's not the case,' I told him.

He was trying to make out that I was so annoyed about not getting justice for the foster parents that I was backing up Laraine's claims just so I could make someone pay.

It was relentless but I was determined not to cry as I didn't want Ryan to know that he could still get to me. I was more angry than upset.

'Debbie, help me with this,' said Mr Collings. 'There is really no plausible explanation, if what you say is true, is there, as to why you and your sister kept going back to that flat?'

'We went back because Alison kept asking us to go up. I went up there 'cos I didn't want Laraine up there on her own with him.'

'But you never chose to report it to anybody, did you?'

'No, I didn't at the time,' I said.

'It simply didn't happen, did it, Debbie?'

'It did happen,' I said, desperate for the cross-examination to be over before I said something I would regret. 'It did. It's all true.'

And thankfully, finally, it was.

'Any more questions for Mrs Grafham, Mr Collings?' asked Judge Tomlinson.

'No, Your Honour,' he said.

'Mrs Grafham, that is the conclusion of your evidence and you are now free to leave court,' the judge told me.

It was such a relief stepping down from that witness box. My legs were like jelly as I walked across the court and I was still shaking.

For once I was glad to be back in the safety of the witness room. Lorna was there and Mum had arrived as she was due to give evidence after me.

'Are you OK?' asked Lorna. 'How did it go?'

'I don't know,' I told her.

'Oh, Debbie, you look like a ghost,' said Mum.

'I'm exhausted,' I said.

'It's no wonder,' said Lorna. 'You've been in there for nearly two hours.'

I still couldn't relax or sit still. I tried to make a cup of tea but my hands were shaking so much, I spilt it everywhere.

'Sit down and take some deep breaths,' Lorna told me.

I was a bag of nerves. The court had broken for lunch and Rob came down to see me. He gave me a big hug.

'Did I do OK?' I said. 'I can't even remember what I said.'

'You were amazing,' he told me. 'You held your own in there and you didn't let him get to you.'

'I'm just worried that it's not going to be enough,' I said.

I was a wreck. I was mentally and physically exhausted. I'd psyched myself up for this day for so long and now it was over, I was so relieved.

Carol and Jo came down to see me.

'You were absolutely brilliant in there, Debbie,' said Carol. 'I'm so proud of you.'

'I think I'm in shock,' I sighed.

I was desperate for a cigarette but Carol didn't think it was a good idea.

'It's best not to go out just yet as Ryan and his family will all be out there. Wait until they've gone.'

Again, I felt like I was the prisoner, not him.

I wasn't allowed to bring my phone into court and

when I checked it, I realised I'd got two missed calls and over fifteen texts from Laraine.

'I'm just ringing to see how it's going, Deb. I hope you are OK. I love you and I'm thinking of you.'

Her texts all said the same thing.

I knew I couldn't speak to her. For a start there was hardly any signal in the witness room, and as well I was in such a daze that I couldn't speak to anyone. I'd had so many questions fired at me that morning, I didn't think that I could answer any more.

After lunch Mum was due to give evidence. I wasn't allowed to sit in court in case I was called back again.

'You can go home now you know, Debbie,' Carol told me. 'You don't have to be here now you've given your evidence.'

'There's no way I'm going anywhere,' I said.

Even if it meant sitting in that witness room for hours on end, I was determined I was going to be there every single day that court was sitting.

Mum was back in fifteen minutes.

Next up was Wendy, who was now Ryan's wife, and then Michael and Shayne's dad. I didn't know why they had been called. I knew Rob didn't want to discuss things in great detail with me as he was terrified about jeopardising the case.

'How do you think it's going?' I said. 'Do you think the jury believes us?'

'It's so hard to call it,' said Rob. 'Nothing's certain.'

I knew he didn't want to get my hopes up. It was a relief when court finally finished for the day. Rob and I waited in the witness room for half an hour for Ryan and his family to leave the court. When we thought the coast was clear, we headed up to the Tesco's, where Rob's dad was waiting.

We were just walking up the road away from the court when I saw who was walking towards us.

'I don't bloody believe it,' I said, sighing as I saw the hunched figure of Patrick Ryan approaching us on the pavement. He was with a younger woman.

'Just put your head down and keep going,' said Rob.

I could see he was worried that there was going to be a big scene. For once, I did as Rob said. I looked at the floor and kept on walking. I held my breath as Ryan passed us. Nobody said a word.

But when he'd gone past I couldn't resist turning round to look at him. Ryan had done exactly the same thing too and for a split second we glared at each other.

'Get in the car, Debbie,' said Rob.

As I sat there and watched Ryan walk away, I realised I was shaking. Even though he was just a pathetic old man he still had the ability to scare me.

'I can't wait to make him pay for what he's done,' I said.

I rang Laraine as soon as we got home.

'Lal, I was in pieces,' I said. 'All those questions and the way that barrister was making out that we were lying. It was just so hard.'

'Well, we've had our day in court,' she said. 'Now it's up to the jury whether they believe us or not.'

'I want him convicted,' I said. 'That's all I'll be happy with. I want him convicted.'

The next day there was no court because we'd been told Ryan had to go for an urgent dressing change on his eye. But Friday we were back there. I knew I'd have to spend all day in the witness room but I didn't care. Ryan was giving evidence that day and I wanted Rob to be in there to hear what he said. Both he and Carol came out smiling.

'All I can say, Debbie, is he hasn't done himself any favours in there,' she said.

'He didn't do very well,' agreed Rob. 'He completely lost it at one point.'

As expected, he said, Ryan had denied that the abuse had ever happened. He'd told the court that he worked away a lot as a carpet fitter and he was only ever there at weekends and then Wendy was around.

'What a liar!' I said. 'I hope the jury see through it.'

It was a good job that I'd insisted on staying at court as on Friday afternoon I was suddenly called back in. I had no idea what I was going to be asked when I took the stand.

'Mrs Grafham, the court has heard how you were sexually assaulted by your father around the same time as you allege the abuse with Mr Ryan started,' said Mr Collings.

'Yes, that's right,' I told him.

'Is there any way that you could have mistaken Mr Ryan for your father? That you could have confused the two men?'

I knew he was just clutching at straws now.

'My father abused me once and it was in my bed, downstairs in our flat,' I said. 'When Ryan done it, it was up in his flat and it happened around twenty times over several years. I think I know the difference between them both.'

That was it. I was only in the witness box for a couple of minutes and I was allowed to go again.

As usual, Laraine rang me that night for an update.

'How do you think it's going, Deb?'

'I just don't know,' I told her. 'I don't dare get my hopes up.'

We'd both gone in there and told the truth and now it was down to twelve strangers to decide whether to believe us or not.

That night Rob and I went back to Eastbourne for the weekend. It was so nice to see the children and it was the one place where I felt safe. I was exhausted by everything that had happened and dreading the week ahead as I knew the jury were likely to come back with their verdict at some point. I felt so guilty as it was Vicky's eighteenth birthday on the following Tuesday and Ryan had even managed to spoil that.

'Whatever happens, we'll come back home that night and take you out for dinner,' I told her.

But I was dreading it as I didn't know what was going to happen. Would the jury have come back by then? Would I even feel like celebrating?

I went back up to London that Sunday evening with a heavy heart. Laraine and I had spoken and texted every single day.

This is the week his fate finally gets decided, I told her.

Just the thought of it made me feel ill. As expected, on Monday morning Judge Tomlinson did his summing-up.

Rob came back at lunchtime, and said: 'The jury's been sent out to consider its verdict.'

The waiting began. Rob, Lorna and I spent all day in the witness room, pacing up and down.

'This is unbearable,' I said. 'I wonder what they're all thinking in there. They can't believe him, they just can't.'

I had butterflies in my stomach and I felt sick that twelve strangers were now in a room nearby deciding whether Laraine and I were telling the truth.

Laraine kept texting me.

Any news? What's happening?

I don't think it's going to be today, I texted back.

It wasn't. The jury came back at 4pm and said they hadn't reached a verdict, so the court was discharged for the day.

The waiting was horrendous. I couldn't eat a thing and neither Rob nor I slept that night. On Tuesday morning, I phoned Vicky before I went to court.

'Happy birthday, love,' I said. 'Whatever happens, we'll see you tonight.'

'Good luck, Mum,' she said.

But I knew that if Ryan was not found guilty today there was no way I would be able to go out celebrating that evening.

We got to court just after 10am. We'd prepared ourselves for another long wait in the witness room but just before 11am, an announcement came over the tannoy system.

'Will all parties in the case of Patrick Ryan please return to court one.'

Rob and I looked at each other.

'It can't be,' he said. 'I'll go down to the court to check what's going on.'

He'd been gone five minutes when Carol rushed in.

'Debbie, the jury have come back,' she said. 'It's the verdict.'

I couldn't believe what I was hearing. I didn't know whether it was a good or a bad thing that they'd come back so quickly.

'Come on,' she said. 'We've got to get back to court.'

But I was suddenly filled with panic. I wasn't ready for this.

'No, I can't,' I said. 'I don't want to go. I can't face it.'

'Come on, Debbie,' she told me. 'This is the moment you've been waiting for.'

She practically had to drag me out of the witness room and into the court.

At first, the police weren't going to allow me in court at all for the reading of the verdict. Even the judge had advised that it was a bad idea for me to be present because of all Ryan's supporters. They were worried that whatever the verdict was, things were going to kick off. In the end Mr Williams had got special permission for me to be there.

'You, Rob and Lorna can all sit in the press benches in the well of the court so you're well away from Ryan's family in the public gallery,' Carol told us.

Rob and Lorna were already sat there when Carol and I walked in.

'Remember, Debbie, if the first count comes back not guilty then it doesn't necessarily mean they're all going to be the same,' she warned me.

But in my mind, it was all or nothing. The jury either believed Laraine and I or they didn't.

They brought Ryan in and he was told to stand up in the dock. As usual he showed no reaction. The foreman of the jury – the man in his fifties in a smart suit – stood up.

'Have you reached a verdict?' Judge Tomlinson asked him.

'Yes, Your Honour,' he said.

'On the first count of rape do you find the defendant guilty or not guilty?'

I closed my eyes and squeezed Rob's hand. I didn't move, I didn't even dare to breathe.

'Guilty, Your Honour.'

I opened my eyes and gasped. Rob threw his arms around me. Lorna burst into tears and even Carol was crying.

As the judge went through each charge, every single one came back 'guilty'.

I was numb. I just stood there, completely gobsmacked. I didn't feel like crying or celebrating.

'I just can't believe it,' I sighed.

I looked over at Ryan in the dock and he was shaking his head as he was taken down to custody. I could hear his family up in the public gallery, shouting and hammering on the glass. But I didn't care.

They'd found him guilty. Guilty of every single charge.

'They believed us,' I said to Rob.

'Of course they did,' he replied, tears streaming down his face. 'I'm so proud of you, Deb.'

It was such a huge relief.

'Debbie, I've never known anything like it,' said Carol, giving me a hug. 'For every charge in an historic abuse case like yours to come back guilty is just amazing. You and Laraine should be so proud of yourselves.'

But I didn't feel proud. I was just in shock.

I sat there, stunned, as the judge left the courtroom and the jury filed out.

'Thank you so much,' Rob shouted across to each of them as they left.

That was it. It was over.

'I think it's a good idea for you to stay in the witness

protection room for a while until Ryan's family have left the court,' Jo told us.

All I wanted was to get as far away from that court as possible. I wanted to have a cigarette and then go back home and see my daughter on her birthday.

There was hardly any signal in the witness room but Rob managed to text my mum, his dad and the kids.

'What about Laraine?' I said to Carol.

'Jo's gone to phone her,' she said. 'And we're going to go round and see her now and check she's all right.'

Two hours later we finally left the court. As I walked out of that place, I felt like the weight of the world had been lifted from my shoulders.

'We've done it,' I said to Rob. 'Me and Laraine have made that bastard pay after all this time.'

I knew then that the one person I wanted to be with right now was her. I needed to see my sister.

Chapter 20
Moving On

I typed the number in the keypad and the front door opened.

'Laraine,' I yelled. 'We're here!'

Before I could go into the bedroom to see her, Carol and Jo came out.

'We're just going,' said Carol. 'We'll leave you two to have some time together on your own.

'Laraine's very emotional, so I think it will do her good to see you.'

'I'll wait out here,' said Rob.

So far I hadn't cried but the minute I walked into Laraine's bedroom and saw her lying there, I broke down. It was as if all the stress and emotion of the past few months came tumbling out. I didn't have to be strong any more or put on a brave face because I was with the one other person who knew exactly how I felt.

She was crying, too.

I put my arms around her and gave her a hug.

'We did it, Lal.' I smiled, tears streaming down my face. 'We did it! We got him.'

'I still can't believe it,' she said. 'I didn't ever dare think they'd find him guilty but they believed us, Deb.'

That was the thing that meant so much after all this time. Despite everything Ryan had always said to us, twelve strangers had believed that we were telling the truth and it was such a relief.

I lay down on the double bed next to Laraine. We were both in shock about the verdict and completely overwhelmed.

'It doesn't feel real to me,' I told her. 'It feels like I'm in a daze.'

'I know,' she said. 'I can't believe after all these years that it's done. We can finally move on.'

But unlike Laraine, it didn't feel like it was over to me. This court case had been my focus for so long, my life had literally been on hold for the past few years and I couldn't quite believe that it had ended. I didn't feel ready to move on yet.

'There's still the sentencing,' I told her. 'I hope they lock him away and they throw away the key.'

But sadly I knew that was unlikely to be the case. Carol had already warned me that he might only get a couple of years.

'We should be celebrating,' said Laraine. 'I'd have a drink if I knew it wasn't going to kill me.'

'How about a cup of tea and a sandwich instead?' I smiled.

We sat on the bed together and ate a ham sandwich.

'I'm really going to miss Carol and Jo,' she told me. 'I got really upset having to say goodbye.'

'Me too,' I said. 'But we'll stay in touch and I'll see them at court for the sentencing.'

We spent two hours chatting and laughing. It felt so nice to be normal again, not worrying about the latest development in the court case or being terrified about the trial, or frightened of discussing anything in our statements. That shadow hanging over us for so long had gone. I hated leaving her but I knew I had to.

'I'm really sorry but I've got to go now,' I said.

'When are you coming back?' she asked. 'Will you come and see me tomorrow?'

'Lal, we're going back to Eastbourne now,' I said. 'I just want to go home and see my little girl for her birthday.'

All I wanted to do was get on that train and go home, far away from London and all the memories of Patrick Ryan.

'I love you and I'm so proud of you,' I told her, giving her a kiss.

'Love you too,' she said. 'I couldn't have done this without you, Deb.'

Laraine started to cry again. It was so hard to leave her but I knew we had to head back.

When we got home to Eastbourne, the kids were waiting for us. They all gave me a cuddle when I walked in, which set me off again.

'We're so proud of you, Mum,' said Vicky.

'Thank you for standing by me,' I told them. 'I know that I've been horrendous to live with but hopefully things can get back to normal again.'

But I still felt far from normal. One of the first things I did when I got home was to have a boiling hot bath, then a shower and then another bath. Just seeing Ryan in court again had made me feel so dirty and humiliated and I was in the bathroom for hours. Every night after a day in court I'd done exactly the same thing. It was as if I was trying to physically scrub away the shame.

That night a big group of us went out for Vicky's eighteenth birthday meal to an American diner but I didn't feel like celebrating. I still couldn't believe that it had happened, it didn't feel real.

'I don't want anyone to mention the court case,' I told Rob.

This was Vicky's night and I didn't want to overshadow it. But I was mentally and physically exhausted. I only had two glasses of wine and I wanted to go home.

Now that Patrick Ryan had been found guilty, life should have got back to normal but I still couldn't rest. My obsession for over a year had been the court case and now it was the sentencing. Every day I phoned Jo and Carol to see if they had any news.

'Do you know when it's going to be?' I kept asking.

'It's hopefully happening some time in May but we haven't got a date yet,' Carol told me.

I was also worried about how long he was going to get.

Finally, Carol texted to say the date had been set for 31 May 2013. But a few days later she rang to say it had been deferred until 4 June.

'Why's that?' I said. 'Oh God, has he appealed?'

'Debbie, it's only been deferred by a few days because Judge Tomlinson is on holiday that week,' Carol told me.

It was a valid reason but I felt so anxious that the news sent me completely off the rails. I'd been trying to cut down on alcohol but I sat there all day after Carol had called, downing drink after drink.

All sorts of silly things were running through my mind. What if it had been adjourned because they thought the jury had made a mistake and he wasn't really guilty? What if he only got a couple of years? That would mean he would be out in a few months on good behaviour. How could I rest, knowing that Ryan was walking the streets, a free man?

Without thinking, I staggered into the kitchen and picked the biggest knife that I could find in the rack. I took it into the conservatory and sat on the sofa, running my fingers along the cold metal of the blade.

I thought about Patrick Ryan and all he had done to Laraine and I and how he had ruined our lives.

'I hate you,' I said out loud.

He had to pay – or I would make him. I raised the knife and plunged it into the arm of the leather sofa, again and again, until my hands ached. Suddenly I looked up and saw a figure in the sliding doors that led through to the living room. It was my son Daniel. He was watching me through the glass and I could see the fear in his eyes as he noticed the carving knife in my hand.

'Daniel, it's OK,' I shouted. 'I'm not going to do anything.'

But he ran off. He must have gone upstairs to tell Rob because he came rushing in.

'Debbie, what the hell are you doing?' he said. 'Please put the knife down.'

A few minutes later I heard sirens outside the house.

'I'm sorry I had to call 999,' he said. 'I was worried you were going to hurt yourself.'

He opened the door and two police officers and a paramedic came running in. I just sat there on the sofa, holding the knife.

'You need to come with us, Mrs Grafham,' a policewoman told me.

'I'm not coming,' I slurred. 'I've not hurt nobody.'

'I'm afraid for your own safety you need to come with us,' she repeated.

'You can piss off,' I said.

The next thing I knew, she'd snatched the knife from my hands. My arms were twisted behind my back and a pair of handcuffs were slapped around my wrists.

'You ain't taking me anywhere!' I yelled.

'It's for your own safety,' the policewoman said, marching me outside to where a police van was waiting.

As we pulled away, I saw Daniel's worried face at the front window. What must he have been thinking to see his mum in such a state being dragged out by the police?

I was taken to the police pound in Eastbourne, where I was put in a cell.

'You can stay in there and sleep it off,' the officer told me.

'You might have taken my knife but if I really want to kill myself then there's nothing you can do to stop me!' I shouted.

It was a stupid thing to say because the next minute she'd stripped me of all my clothes. I sat there, shivering, with nothing but a scratchy grey blanket.

The cell had a stone wall and floor and it was absolutely freezing. There was a bed built into the wall with a paper-thin mattress, a desk and a toilet in the corner as well as a video camera so that I could be monitored at all times.

I was absolutely furious. I was desperate to get out of there and have a cigarette.

'I ain't done nothing, you can't keep me here!' I yelled. 'I've got to go to court next week.'

I hammered on the door for so long my knuckles were bleeding and red raw.

I couldn't sleep because I was so cold. Eventually in the early hours of the morning when I'd sobered up, two psychiatric nurses came to assess me. Thankfully, they decided that it had been the alcohol talking and I wasn't a danger to myself so they agreed to let me go.

A police van dropped me home at 6am. Understandably, Rob was furious.

'This has got to stop, Debbie,' he said. 'I know you've been to hell and back with the court case but this family can't take much more.

'We need to try and put this behind us and move on.'

I knew he was right. I was destroying my marriage, my relationship with my children.

'I'm sorry,' I said. 'Once the sentencing is over with I promise I'll get back on track.'

It couldn't come soon enough for me.

On 4 June 2013 Rob and I got the train up to London for the sentencing. As I walked up to Woolwich Crown Court, I felt nervous as I had last time, but this time around I was almost looking forward to it. We'd got the hard part out of the way and now Ryan was finally going to be punished for what he had done.

Carol and Jo were waiting for us and as always, Lorna had come along for moral support.

'Ryan's family are here in the public gallery, so I think it's best for you three to sit with us in the press bench again,' said Carol.

I felt sick as we took our places in court one. Just being there brought back all the traumatic memories of having to give evidence and be cross-examined. This was the place where everyone had heard my dirty secrets. I was also nervous about how long Ryan was going to get.

'If he gets ten years then I'll be happy,' I told Rob.

'Debbie, you're going to have to accept whatever the judge decides,' he said.

I could see he was worried about the outcome as he knew a short sentence could send me off the rails again.

I stared at the dock as Ryan was brought in, flanked by two security guards. He was wearing the same scruffy navy jumper and shirt underneath, but he looked even older somehow. I was happy to see the effect six weeks in prison had had on him.

As soon as he stepped into the dock, he glared at me.

'We'll start today's proceedings by hearing the victim impact statements,' said Judge Tomlinson.

I listened as Mr Williams, the prosecution barrister, read out mine and Laraine's statements about what effect Patrick Ryan's abuse had had on our lives. It was so hard to hear.

'Both these women have suffered from problems with alcohol and anorexia and have had psychiatric problems,' he said.

'It's affected their ability to form meaningful relationships and how they are with their own children. It's also had a huge financial impact. For the duration of legal proceedings and the trial, Mrs Grafham has been unable to work. As the result of alcohol abuse, Mrs Delgiudice had a long stay in hospital, where she was seriously ill and is now bedbound and completely dependent on carers.'

Tears filled my eyes as I realised how the abuse had changed us both. But I was determined that I wouldn't let Patrick Ryan see me cry.

Then it was time for Judge Tomlinson to pass sentence. Patrick Ryan stood up in the dock.

'There is no doubt that Maureen Fermor and her daughters were vulnerable at this time of their lives,' he said. 'While her mostly estranged husband was serving a prison sentence, Maureen had had a lengthy stay in hospital lasting several months and, after her discharge, she remained on antidepressant medication because of her fragile mental state. Her three children had been in care for about six months and, although Laraine was too young to have any memory of it, there is no doubt in my mind that both these young sisters, Laraine and Deborah, were terrified of ever again being separated from their mother. Their reason for not complaining to her or their teachers at school about this serious abuse committed by you, and which the elder child has disclosed she was subjected to by others, was not difficult to comprehend.'

I stared at Ryan but still he didn't flinch or show any reaction as Judge Tomlinson continued. He just looked at the floor, like the true coward he was.

'You said in evidence that you were frequently away working in Birmingham and would simply not have been around at any time during the weekdays when, according to these children, you subjected them to sustained sexual violence, which they both described in graphic terms.

'I do not regard it as simply an unfortunate coincidence that throughout most of the period covered by the indictment you were serving a lengthy period of disqualification from holding or obtaining a driving licence, a state of affairs that would have substantially curtailed your ability to work away from home, though it may be that you had little respect for court orders.

'The fact remains that this detail is something that neither of these witnesses could possibly have known, particularly as it emerged during your trial almost by chance, and, as I say, I do not regard it as a coincidence.

'Each of these victims had to relive these experiences by giving evidence. Their impact statements make grim reading.

'Laraine's statement, in many ways, replicates the evidence given by her own mother, who described the sort of child she was, and similarly in the case of Deborah she was undoubtedly a very angry child, and the impact of these offences has, of course, seriously undermined their ability to form meaningful relationships in adulthood, though it is clear that they have both in any case turned their lives around and for that they should both be congratulated.'

Rob squeezed my hand and I gave him a weak smile. I knew what was coming next, though, and my heart was pounding.

'Mr Ryan, the sentence that I impose, and it may seem to some to be a lenient sentence, is twelve years' imprisonment.'

It was a lot more that I had been expecting and I was completely stunned. Carol smiled and gave me a big hug.

Judge Tomlinson stood up.

'May I express my admiration to all these witnesses in this case for the way in which they have been able to conduct themselves throughout,' he said before retiring.

I stared over at the dock. I wanted one last look at Patrick Ryan before he was taken down. He caught my eye and glared at me.

'You little fucking c**t!' he shouted.

I was so shocked, I burst into tears.

'That's what he used to call me,' I sobbed to Rob. 'That's what he called me after he raped me.'

'Don't let him get to you,' said Rob.

I was upset, but in a way I was also pleased that at last Ryan had shown some reaction as I knew that finally I had got to him.

Rob had been so good all throughout the trial but this time he couldn't bite his tongue any longer.

'I hope you rot in there!' he shouted over to Ryan.

His own family were shouting and shaking their heads.

'I love you, Dad,' someone in the public gallery yelled as he was led away by the security guards.

And just like that, he was gone. Off to serve his sentence.

'Right, let's get you out of here,' said Carol.

I knew she was worried about the possibility of trouble, so she quickly led us through a coded door at the back of the court. We walked through all these corridors to another witness room. I couldn't get a signal in there.

'What about Laraine?' I said. 'I need to call her.'

'You need to stay here until the coast is clear,' said Jo. 'We'll go and give her a ring to tell her the good news.'

I knew she was going to be ecstatic.

We texted Rob's dad, Mum and the kids.

'Are you pleased?' said Rob.

But I still don't think that it had sunk in.

'I can't believe it,' I said. 'I'm amazed that he got so long.'

But there was still one thing that had really stung. Right up until the end, Ryan had never admitted what he'd done to us or shown any remorse. He'd been so cocky and sure of himself all along.

'Prison's too good for that man,' I said.

We were in the witness room for nearly two hours until it was decided it was safe for us to leave. Walking out of the court for the last time felt strange. We'd done it, this really was the end. This case had consumed me and my life for so long and now it was over. I knew it would take a long time for that to hit home.

It was hard having to say goodbye to Carol and Jo. Even though I'd treated them terribly at times, I knew we wouldn't have got through the court case without them.

'I'm going to miss you,' I told them. 'You've been brilliant.'

'Oh, don't worry, we'll keep in touch. You're on my Christmas card list,' joked Carol.

From the court we went to see Laraine, as I'd promised that we'd call in on the way back. We were both very emotional and upset.

'I'm crying because I'm so relieved,' Laraine told me.

'I'm just in shock,' I said. 'I never expected him to get that long.'

Even though I knew he'd been found guilty it still hadn't really sunk in until that day when I'd heard his sentence. I finally felt safe, knowing he was now locked away. It was only then that I found out details about the abuse Laraine had suffered from Ryan. How he'd already raped her a couple of times by the time I caught him on the landing with her and how he had sexually assaulted her with a screwdriver. No wonder she'd never wanted to talk about it with me.

'I'm so sorry,' I told Laraine. 'I'd no idea of the things he'd done to you.'

'It's OK, it's over,' she sighed. 'It's finally over, Deb.'

It was, but I knew that for me, it was going to take a lot of getting used to.

'Will you come back up and see me soon?' said Laraine.

But I didn't answer. I couldn't, you see, because in my mind I didn't think that I could ever go back there again. One of the reasons I was so emotional was because I felt in a way I was saying goodbye to my sister too.

Every time I went to that part of London to visit Laraine, I'd pass all the places that reminded me of everything that we'd been through – Blackheath, where we'd been abused; Woolwich, where we'd had to face him in court; Greenwich, where we'd moved to afterwards. It was painful for me to see Laraine like that too, stuck in bed, unable to do anything for herself, as it just reminded me of Ryan and what he'd done to our lives.

If I really and truly wanted to move on, I didn't think I could bring myself to go back to that area any more. I didn't say anything to Laraine about how I was feeling as I knew she would be devastated.

'I'll speak to you soon, Lal,' I said, giving her a kiss on the cheek. 'I love you.'

As I closed the door of Laraine's house behind us, I burst into tears.

Chapter 21

Facing My Demons

Now the court case was over I knew I had to get my life back on track otherwise I was going to lose everything – Rob, the kids, my job. It was the reason that I'd started drinking heavily but it was over now, so the alcohol had to stop too.

But I also knew that I couldn't do that on my own without professional help, it had gone too far for that. So I went to see my GP.

'I want to stop drinking,' I told him. 'But I think I need someone to help me.'

I knew after everything that we'd been through with Laraine and David that with the amount I was drinking it was dangerous to stop suddenly. Going cold turkey could lead to seizures or even death.

'We'll try and enrol you on a detox programme where they'll help withdraw you gradually,' he said.

It was going to be hard but I knew I had to do this. To prove I was serious about it, twice a week for six weeks I had to go and have an appointment with a counsellor and a nurse, then they would decide whether I was a suitable candidate for a detox.

My first appointment was at 5pm and to prove how determined I was about it, I didn't have any alcohol all day. But by the time I got there, I was a mess. I was sweating and shaking and I could see Rob was concerned.

'Debbie, are you OK?' he asked. 'You look terrible.'

'How have I let things get this bad?' I said.

It was frightening to see just how dependent on alcohol my body had become. My counsellor, a woman called Ruth, took one look at me and said, 'I know this sounds strange when you're hoping to detox but you need to go and have a drink. There's no way we can talk when you're in such a state.'

I did as she said. Over the next few weeks we talked about everything. There were no more secrets in my life, so I told her all about Patrick Ryan.

'I drunk to help me cope,' I said. 'And the more I drank, the less effect it had, so I just drank more and more.'

'I don't really blame you,' she said. 'You've been through so much.'

It was nice not to feel judged for once.

'That's what drove me to it but now I've got to take responsibility for my own actions,' I said.

I couldn't blame everything on the abuse and I'd managed to stay sober throughout the court case.

'I really want to do this detox,' I said. 'I need to do this for my family and for myself.'

I told everyone what I was doing. I even came clean to Laraine.

'I didn't realise you were drinking so much,' she said. 'Why didn't you tell me before it was this bad?'

'Because I didn't want to worry you,' I told her. 'You had enough on your plate without me adding to your problems.'

She was behind me 100 per cent.

'You can do this, Deb,' she said. 'You don't want to end up like me.'

On Tuesday, 24 July 2013, Rob and Lorna took me to Mill View hospital in Hove. I was due to be in there for a week.

'I don't want you to go and leave me here,' I sobbed. 'I can't do this.'

I was petrified. Just the thought of not being able to have a drink or to be able to buy any alcohol was terrifying and I was scared about being away from my family for so long.

'You can do this, Debbie,' Rob told me. 'You're so strong.'

I knew I had to get through it and in a way, it wasn't as bad as I was expecting. At first I was put on a very high dose of diazepam to cope with the alcohol withdrawal. I was shaky and going hot and cold, but the majority of the time I was so drowsy, I just slept.

The rules in there were very strict. It was a secure unit and all visitors were searched and breathalysed to make sure they weren't bringing any alcohol or drugs in. Someone would escort you to the dining room and the toilet and you weren't even allowed caffeine as it was classed as a stimulant.

I had my own room and thankfully I was allowed to bring my mobile phone in with me. Laraine texted me every day.

How are you doing? Hang on in there. I'm thinking of you xx

Rob came to visit on the Wednesday night but I was so doped up, I don't remember much about it.

The next day he was off work so he brought the children up to see me. We all sat together in a family room and I made sure I was showered and dressed. Daniel was sad that I was going to be away for his fifteenth birthday the following week and I could see Vicky was upset. I knew it was hard for everyone seeing me in there.

'I bought you some nail varnish, Mum, but they took it off me when they searched me on the way in,' she said.

We weren't even allowed that in case we inhaled the vapours.

I found it hard too, and when they were leaving, I started to cry.

'I just wish I could come home with you,' I said.

'Soon, Deb,' said Rob.

As each day passed, I could feel myself getting stronger. In the time leading up to the court case I hadn't eaten properly for weeks and my only calories had been from alcohol. But in there they made me eat and I started to feel a lot better.

You were also encouraged to attend a group therapy session, which I hated.

'Please introduce yourself to the group and if you want, you can talk about the reasons why you're here,' the therapist told me.

But I didn't want to talk to a bunch of strangers about what I'd been through. It felt like being in court all over again and in a way I was fed up of talking about it. Also, I didn't want people to think that I blamed the abuse for my drinking: I'd come to realise that I had done this to myself, not Patrick Ryan.

'I've had a rough year,' I said. 'Things got too much and I couldn't cope with the stress and so I turned to drink.'

I didn't want to say any more.

The sad thing was, from listening to other people's stories, I found out that like me so many of them had been abused as children: both men and women.

In a way it made me feel even more determined to succeed. Sadly, several of them were on their third or fourth detox but I was adamant I was only going to be in there once.

After six days, I was allowed out with a support worker to go to the local supermarket. She followed me around and stood at the end of each aisle as I picked things up. It was a boiling hot summer's day and I was desperate for an ice cream.

'I really fancy a tub,' I told her.

Ironically, my favourite flavour was rum and raisin, but when I picked it up out of the freezer, she shook her head.

'It's just flavouring, it hasn't got any alcohol in it,' I said, but I wasn't allowed it.

I felt like a prisoner.

'I bet Patrick Ryan's got more freedom than this,' I said.

But after a while you got used to it and I felt safe and protected. I was only supposed to be in there for a week but even though I was desperate to get home, I was panicking about how I was going to cope. You weren't allowed to go anywhere on your own and I was worried about being tempted to buy alcohol.

'I don't want to go home,' I told Laraine when I rang her. 'I feel safe in here.'

'I know what you mean,' she said. 'I was exactly like that when I was in rehab. It's like having a security blanket.

'Why don't you ask the doctors if you can stay a bit longer?'

So I did and thankfully they agreed that I could stay another week.

Amazingly, the damage to my body from all the drinking had been minimal. The doctors said my liver was slightly enlarged and my kidneys were struggling to flush out all the toxins from the alcohol, but thankfully because I'd stopped drinking when I did, I hadn't been left with any permanent damage.

'The best-case scenario is if you walk out of here and never have another drink again,' the doctor told me.

I just hoped and prayed that I was strong enough to do that.

Finally, two weeks later, I was discharged. I was terrified.

'I'm so scared of slipping back into my old ways,' I told Laraine.

'You won't, Deb,' she said. 'You can do this.'

But I wasn't so sure. I felt like everyone was on edge and watching me like a hawk.

I was due to start back at work at the beginning of August and I couldn't wait. Work would give me a focus, a reason to get up and out of bed on a morning and stop me from thinking about anything else.

On the day of my first shift I got to Eastbourne General half an hour early. But as I walked towards the hospital doors, I started to have palpitations. I felt that familiar tightening in my chest, my head was spinning and I was struggling to breathe.

All the memories came rushing back. The times I'd been taken there when I'd had too many pills or I couldn't go to the toilet, the days I'd been at work and Carol had rung to tell me about the court case. This place held so many memories.

Calm down, I told myself.

It was over. Things were different now.

I went and sat on a bench outside and took deep breaths until the panic had gone. It was lucky that I'd turned up early as it took me four attempts before I was able to walk through the hospital doors and go up to my ward. But I did it in the end as I knew that I couldn't mess this up. I was really lucky to have a job after the way that I'd behaved and I knew I had to really prove myself.

Going through the court case had changed me as a person. For the first time in my life I wasn't ashamed any more about what Laraine and I had been through.

There had been a reporter from a local London newspaper at the sentencing although Laraine and I weren't allowed to be named for legal reasons. Thankfully, Ryan was and they used his police mug shot along with the story. It was the first time Laraine had seen him.

'He looks exactly the same,' she said. 'I got shivers down my spine when I saw his horrible face and that wonky eye.'

'I think I'd like to speak out about what we've been through,' I told her.

'I don't mind if you think it will help other people,' said Laraine.

So I rang the local paper and we both agreed to waive our anonymity and speak out about the abuse we'd suffered at the hands of Patrick Ryan.

I think we were both shocked, though, when it made the front page of *The Eastbourne Herald*.

'Justice after being raped by the monster upstairs,' said the headline.

I was in my local Tesco's a day later when a woman came up to me by the tills.

'You don't know me,' she said. 'But are you the lady who was in the newspaper?'

'Yes,' I said, worried about what she was going to say.

Her eyes filled with tears.

'It happened to me too when I was a girl,' she said. 'I never told anyone but reading your story, I wish I had.'

'It's never too late to get justice,' I said. 'My sister and I didn't think we stood a chance after all those years but we got him in the end.'

'Well done,' she said. 'You must be really proud of yourselves.'

I hadn't thought about that before but she was right: I was proud of all Laraine and I had achieved. I was amazed by how many people, both men and women, came up and congratulated me after reading the story.

'Really well done,' a taxi driver told me. 'I don't know how you did it.'

* * *

So that's why I'm speaking out now. If I can stop the same thing happening to someone else, at least something positive can come out of what Laraine and I went through. And in my opinion, the more people who know about Patrick Ryan, the better.

The abuse I suffered as a child changed me. It made me become a person that I didn't really like – aggressive, hostile, argumentative. I didn't feel proud of myself at the time but I'm beginning to now. I don't have any regrets. In a way I wish we had told someone when we were kids, but I now know how traumatic it is going through a court case and to do that as a child would be very hard. As an adult, I had the strength to do it and not have to hide behind screens. I wasn't glad when Laraine put the wheels in motion but once she had, I couldn't stand back and let her do it on her own. It would have been her word against his. The only way we could have done it was together.

I don't think I'll ever get over the abuse I suffered but I have learned to live with it now. There's still not a day that goes by when I don't think about the foster parents, my father and Patrick Ryan and what they did to me, but it doesn't drive me to destruction any more. I'm still having counselling and that really helps too.

I don't want pity or sympathy or for people to feel sorry for me. I don't want to be a victim any more. I just hope that mine and Laraine's story inspires other people and helps them to do what we did. Even if you go through absolute hell, it's worth it in the end.

Everything is out in the open now and it's such a huge relief that Patrick Ryan is safely behind bars. Even though he was sentenced to twelve years, he's eligible for parole in June 2019. He'll still be on police licence for the following six years as well as being on the Sex Offender's Register. He'll be in his early seventies when he comes out of prison and I hope he won't have much of a life left.

Laraine and I are still fighting our demons. She's still bedbound and the more time that passes, the more frightened she is of trying to be mobile again. I'm still struggling to stay away from alcohol. I've done it but it's not been easy. I've been invited on nights out but haven't gone because I was worried I'd be tempted to have a drink. We used to have people round but we don't any more as Rob's scared they might bring some wine. It's a constant battle.

Just before Christmas I'd had a bad day at work and I found myself buying a bottle of white wine. I didn't drink it, I just hid it in the wardrobe. But a few days later Rob found it.

'Debbie, I can't take much more of this,' he said. 'If you start drinking again, I'm leaving.'

He stormed off out to clear his head.

Well, if he's going to leave I may as well have a drink, I told myself. So I sat on the bed and started to drink it straight from the bottle.

Then Louise came in and found me. Understandably she was so upset.

'I can't do this any more,' I told her, bursting into tears.

'Come on, Mum,' she said, taking my hand.

We went downstairs and I watched while she tipped the rest of the wine down the sink.

I've haven't had a drop since and I'm determined it's going to stay that way. I've seen the damage alcohol did to my brother and sister and I can't do that to myself.

Laraine and I talk every day, either on the phone or we message or text each other, but I'm ashamed to admit that I haven't been back to visit her since the sentencing.

'Deb, why won't you come and see me?' she asks.

I always use the excuse of work or not being able to afford the train ticket. The truth is, it's still too raw, too painful. That area of southeast London holds too many bad memories.

I know that one day, for Laraine's sake, I will go back. But I'm hoping that she and her family will move down to Eastbourne to be near us. It would be a new start for her and it would mean I could see her every day.

I'm still so angry with Patrick Ryan and I hate him. When I look at my sister and how her life is, I know that he's to blame for that. Laraine drank to try and forget what he'd done to her but in the end she couldn't. It breaks my heart to see her unable to even get out of bed at the age of forty-four.

Our relationship has had its ups and downs. We've been to hell and back but we're both still here to tell the tale and we'll always have an unbreakable bond. We both understand what the other has been through, and together we stood strong and showed Patrick Ryan that he wasn't going to win and we weren't going to be victims any more.

I love you, Laraine. We did it, we won! Finally, there are no more secrets.

Acknowledgements

Thank you to my husband Rob and our children – Vicky, Louise and Daniel. You're my life. You've put up with such a lot and I love you all so much. To Mum, for always being there for me. To DC Joanne Crockford and PC Carol Day, thank you for believing in us and helping make sure that we got justice after all those years. You've shown me it's never too late to speak out. Thank you to my counsellor, Lorna Earls, who has helped me in so many ways and gone above and beyond the call of duty so many times. I couldn't, and wouldn't, have done this without you.

Thanks also to Sara Cywinski from Ebury Press for giving me the opportunity to write this book. Finally, thanks to my ghostwriter, Heather Bishop. Without you, this would have been impossible. Thank you for everything.